Ansible Quick Start Guide

Control and monitor infrastructures of any size,
physical or virtual

Mohamed Alibi

BIRMINGHAM - MUMBAI

Ansible Quick Start Guide

Commissioning Editor: Gebin George
Acquisition Editor: Reshma Raman
Content Development Editor: Mohammed Yusuf Imaratwale
Technical Editor: Sushmeeta Jena
Copy Editor: Safis Editing
Project Coordinator: Hardik Bhinde
Proofreader: Safis Editing
Indexer: Tejal Daruwale Soni
Graphics: Alishon Mendonsa
Production Coordinator: Deepika Naik

First published: September 2018

Production reference: 1270918

Published by Packt Publishing Ltd.
Livery Place
35 Livery Street
Birmingham
B3 2PB, UK.

ISBN 978-1-78953-293-7

www.packtpub.com

`mapt.io`

Mapt is an online digital library that gives you full access to over 5,000 books and videos, as well as industry leading tools to help you plan your personal development and advance your career. For more information, please visit our website.

Why subscribe?

- Spend less time learning and more time coding with practical eBooks and Videos from over 4,000 industry professionals

- Improve your learning with Skill Plans built especially for you

- Get a free eBook or video every month

- Mapt is fully searchable

- Copy and paste, print, and bookmark content

Packt.com

Did you know that Packt offers eBook versions of every book published, with PDF and ePub files available? You can upgrade to the eBook version at `www.packt.com` and as a print book customer, you are entitled to a discount on the eBook copy. Get in touch with us at `customercare@packtpub.com` for more details.

At `www.packt.com`, you can also read a collection of free technical articles, sign up for a range of free newsletters, and receive exclusive discounts and offers on Packt books and eBooks.

Contributors

About the author

Mohamed Alibi is a Linux system administrator who works at the European Bioinformatics Institute, EMBL-EBI. His area of specialization is mass virtual machine and container provisioning and infrastructure administration for medium-sized distributed bioinformatics training facilities. He always keeps abreast of the latest innovations and developments in new technologies to solve his daily challenges. He holds an MSc in Networking and Computer Sciences in a collaborative program with the University of Illinois Urbana-Champaign and the IPT of Tunis, where he expanded his expertise in grid computing data management between the NCSA and IGB under the NIH project H3ABioNet. He published his first book in 2015 with Packt, called *Mastering CentOS 7 Linux Server*.

I want to thank my wife, Sabrine, and daughter, Bayah Khadija, for their motivation throughout this journey. I want to thank my friends for supporting me with encouragement and guiding wisdom. I also want to express my deepest gratitude to my colleagues and supervisors for their guidance and continuous support that helped me to achieve my goals. Finally, my deep and sincere gratitude to my family for their continuous and unparalleled love, help, and support.

About the reviewer

Anis Regaieg is an IT infrastructure and cloud computing engineer currently working as a system administrator at the Tunisian Electoral Management Body. With more than five years of experience in Linux system administration, virtualization, and cloud computing, his main expertise is in high availability and performance optimization solutions. Anis is also passionate about new technologies and software programming.

Packt is searching for authors like you

If you're interested in becoming an author for Packt, please visit `authors.packtpub.com` and apply today. We have worked with thousands of developers and tech professionals, just like you, to help them share their insight with the global tech community. You can make a general application, apply for a specific hot topic that we are recruiting an author for, or submit your own idea.

Table of Contents

Preface

This is an Ansible guidebook for beginner systems administrators. It aims to
properly introduce Ansible as an automation and configuration management tool. Readers
of the book should, by the end, master basic use of Ansible playbooks and modules by
learning from real-life sample codes that demonstrate each module's functionality to help
achieve infrastructure and task automation and orchestration. The book contains some
extra advanced tips for those who want to go the extra mile and learn about and collaborate
with the Ansible community.

Who this book is for

This book is for three major audiences. First, systems administrators who work with either
Linux, Windows, or Mac OS X. This covers those who work on bare-metal machines,
virtual infrastructure, or cloud-based environments. Then, network administrators, those
who work on distributed proprietary network equipment. Finally, DevOps. This book
offers a good understanding of how the system they are going to deploy their application in
will behave, enabling them to code accordingly or suggest modifications that can benefit
their applications.

What this book covers

Chapter 1, *What is Ansible?*, is an introduction to Ansible and compares it with other
configuration management tools.

Chapter 2, *Ansible Setup and Configuration*, explains how to set up and configure Ansible on
multiple systems.

Chapter 3, *Ansible Inventory and Playbook*, is an introduction to and overview of Ansible
Inventory and Playbook.

Chapter 4, *Ansible Modules*, covers Ansible's most often used modules with real-life sample
usage code.

Chapter 5, *Ansible Automated Infrastructure*, enumerates Ansible's use cases for multiple
infrastructures.

Chapter 6, *Ansible Coding for Configuration Management*, contains best practices for coding
Ansible playbooks.

Chapter 7, *Ansible Galaxy and Community Roles*, is an introduction to Ansible community roles, usage, and contribution.

Chapter 8, *Ansible Advanced Features*, is an overview of some of Ansible's advanced features, such as Vault, plugins, and containers.

To get the most out of this book

Before reading this book, you should have a basic understanding of the Linux shell and some system administration skills in order to be able to follow the practical examples. Also, some basic coding skills will be very handy when dealing with YAML playbooks. As an optional requirement, having some basic knowledge of configuration management will help to simplify many points in the book.

To be able to run most of the code, we recommend having a virtual environment running at least two Linux machines, a Windows machine, and a Mac OS X. For network device testing, you may need a test network device or some virtual network equipment.

Download the example code files

You can download the example code files for this book from your account at www.packt.com. If you purchased this book elsewhere, you can visit www.packt.com/support and register to have the files emailed directly to you.

You can download the code files by following these steps:

1. Log in or register at www.packt.com.
2. Select the **SUPPORT** tab.
3. Click on **Code Downloads & Errata**.
4. Enter the name of the book in the **Search** box and follow the onscreen instructions.

Once the file is downloaded, please make sure that you unzip or extract the folder using the latest version of:

- WinRAR/7-Zip for Windows
- Zipeg/iZip/UnRarX for Mac
- 7-Zip/PeaZip for Linux

The code bundle for the book is also hosted on GitHub at
`https://github.com/PacktPublishing/Ansible-Quick-Start-Guide`. In case there's an
update to the code, it will be updated on the existing GitHub repository.

We also have other code bundles from our rich catalog of books and videos available
at `https://github.com/PacktPublishing/`. Check them out!

Download the color images

We also provide a PDF file that has color images of the screenshots/diagrams used in this
book. You can download it here:
`https://www.packtpub.com/sites/default/files/downloads/9781789532937_ColorImage`
`s.pdf`.

Conventions used

There are a number of text conventions used throughout this book.

`CodeInText`: Indicates code words in text, database table names, folder names, filenames,
file extensions, pathnames, dummy URLs, user input, and Twitter handles. Here is an
example: "Mount the downloaded `WebStorm-10*.dmg` disk image file as another disk in
your system."

A block of code is set as follows:

```
$link =
"https://raw.githubusercontent.com/ansible/ansible/devel/examples/scripts/C
onfigureRemotingForAnsible.ps1"
$script = "$env:temp\ConfigureRemotingForAnsible.ps1"

(New-Object -TypeName System.Net.WebClient).DownloadFile($link, $script)
```

When we wish to draw your attention to a particular part of a code block, the relevant lines
or items are set in bold:

```
$link =
"https://raw.githubusercontent.com/ansible/ansible/devel/examples/scripts/C
onfigureRemotingForAnsible.ps1"
$script = "$env:temp\ConfigureRemotingForAnsible.ps1"

(New-Object -TypeName System.Net.WebClient).DownloadFile($link, $script)
```

Any command-line input or output is written as follows:

```
sudo apt install -y expect
```

Bold: Indicates a new term, an important word, or words that you see onscreen. For example, words in menus or dialog boxes appear in the text like this. Here is an example: "Select **System info** from the **Administration** panel."

Warnings or important notes appear like this.

Tips and tricks appear like this.

Get in touch

Feedback from our readers is always welcome.

General feedback: If you have questions about any aspect of this book, mention the book title in the subject of your message and email us at customercare@packtpub.com.

Errata: Although we have taken every care to ensure the accuracy of our content, mistakes do happen. If you have found a mistake in this book, we would be grateful if you would report this to us. Please visit www.packt.com/submit-errata, selecting your book, clicking on the Errata Submission Form link, and entering the details.

Piracy: If you come across any illegal copies of our works in any form on the Internet, we would be grateful if you would provide us with the location address or website name. Please contact us at copyright@packt.com with a link to the material.

If you are interested in becoming an author: If there is a topic that you have expertise in and you are interested in either writing or contributing to a book, please visit authors.packtpub.com.

Reviews

Please leave a review. Once you have read and used this book, why not leave a review on the site that you purchased it from? Potential readers can then see and use your unbiased opinion to make purchase decisions, we at Packt can understand what you think about our products, and our authors can see your feedback on their book. Thank you!

For more information about Packt, please visit `packt.com`.

1
What is Ansible?

Following the first industrial revolution, automation was introduced, making the already-efficient machinery that had been developed even more efficient. This led to the introduction of industrial constructions, vehicle steering and stabilization, and indoor environmental control, among many other developments. After this, the information revolution kicked in, initiating a new process of optimization. This phase is working to reduce human intervention in technological processes and raise productivity.

Nowadays, automation has become the norm across all fields. It started with simple administrator scripts, written to simplify and speed up daily tasks, and quickly developed into fully-fledged configuration management tools. The reasons behind this rapid development were the increase in market demand, the expansion of infrastructure and applications, and the emergence of new technologies, such as continuous integration, continuous development, and machine provisioning, that require a much more complicated setup and configuration.

By nature, systems and network administrators tend to want to reduce repetitive tasks, simplify complicated ones, and try to move on to the next task as quickly as possible. At first, there were a few simple scripts, such as Bash or PowerShell, that were able to optimize tasks in a standard environment. After that, longer and more complicated scripts that involved advanced programming languages such as Python or Ruby were developed. These aimed to address tasks across multiple platforms or in complex environments and to manage infrastructure using automation and orchestration tools, enabling businesses to grow dramatically overnight with more demanding and complicated services. The role of administrators is to manage this growth and act accordingly to ensure a seamless user experience.

This chapter will provide an overview of Ansible. We will demonstrate that Ansible is now a must-have platform for managing a medium to large infrastructure, rather than having a physical, partially virtual or hybrid, private and public cloud. Other automation tools offer different benefits with regard to their installation, usage, speed, and flexibility, so it can be tricky for a first-time user to choose the most appropriate automation tool for their environment. Ansible, Chef, Puppet, and SaltStack are the major configuration management tools available on the market. Each of these follows a different method of deploying, configuring, and managing machines with reduced complexity and increased speed, reliability, and compliance. This chapter will cover the following topics:

- Market study of automation tools
- Introduction to Ansible as a configuration management and task orchestration tool
- Exploration of Ansible's functionalities across operating systems, architectures, and cloud platforms
- Overview of the Ansible project and Tower

The IT configuration management market

The major configuration management tools currently used in the market are Ansible, Chef, Puppet, and SaltStack. Each one of these has their own pros and cons, so finding the right one can be a bit challenging, depending on which features are valued or which programming language is preferred. In this section, we will briefly introduce each of the tools and explain why we have chosen Ansible in this book.

Chef is an open source, client-server configuration management tool. It offers a flexible infrastructure automation framework using Ruby and **domain-specific language** (**DSL**) for the administration of hosts. This covers all types of hosts, including bare metal, virtual, or on the cloud. Chef is very common with code developers due to its flexibility, stability, and reliability in large cloud deployments. However, it can be challenging to set up and learn its functionalities, so it might take a new user some time before properly mastering it.

Puppet is a Ruby-based configuration management and orchestration tool. It follows an agent/master architecture, where the hosts to be controlled require a Puppet agent to allow their management. Puppet features a strong automation and reporting capability, via its UI interface, for task submission and host real-time reporting. Like Chef, Puppet can be challenging for new users to set up and configure. A prior knowledge of Ruby and DSL is required to perform personalized and complex tasks.

Puppet and Chef are two of the oldest configuration management platforms. They both use Ruby and DSL to control their agents.

SaltStack is a Python-coded platform built to allow high-speed, master-agent communication. Its configuration management tasks are coded in **Yet Another Markdown Language (YAML)**. The master (or multiple masters) uses the SSH protocol to control the agents/minions. SaltStack is very scalable, meaning it can respond well to environmental changes, it is easy to use, and it has a strong community. On the other hand, its installation can be difficult for a new user, its UI is not well-developed, it focuses on Linux with an average cover of other operating systems, and its documentation lacks good management.

SaltStack is very similar to Ansible. They both employ easy-to-use coding languages, that is, Python and YAML. Also, both SaltStack and Ansible execute tasks very quickly because they rely on SSH to send comments to the hosts.

Ansible is a relatively new tool compared to the others. It was built to simplify the complexity of task automation and orchestration. It is built on Python and uses YAML for scripting its jobs, which is a language that is very simple and close to English. This allows new users to understand it easily and write it themselves. Ansible does not require an agent to be installed in the hosts. It supports both push and pull models to send commands to its Linux nodes via the SSH protocol, and the WinRM protocol to send commands to its Windows nodes. It allows for a seamless deployment and provisioning for both VMs, applications, and containers, and scales easily to match the environment growth. It is simple to install and configure, and it is fairly easy to learn how to use it and code its scripts. Ansible does not require agent installation, which improves its communication speed. It is predominantly advanced in configuration management tasks, but it can also behave as an infrastructure orchestration tool. However, it requires extra permission for the master nodes. Users can easily end up with multiple scripts for multiple tasks, which can get confusing, and it lacks a good GUI and a mature platform when compared to older tools.

Each of these tools is built for a specific audience. They have many well-developed features to cover a user's unique requirements to either simplify their daily tasks, improve productivity, speed up a host configuration, or close the gap in a hybrid environment.

We have chosen to cover Ansible in this book to make it future-proof. We can all agree that Ansible is a new platform, so it is not as well-designed and customizable as many of the other tools, but it is easy to see how fast Ansible is on the rise. We are not just talking about the number of new technologies it supports, the number of modules it is introducing and enhancing, the community support that is present on the Ansible Galaxy form, or the GitHub project forks and starred repositories. We are also following its popularity and its demand within the market.

 Red Hat acquired Ansible in October 2015 with the strong belief that Ansible is the leader in IT automation and DevOps delivery, with the ability to simplify management for hybrid clouds, OpenStack environments, and container-based services.

"Ansible is a clear leader in IT automation and DevOps, and helps Red Hat take a significant step forward in our goal of creating frictionless IT."

– Joe Fitzgerald, Vice President, Management, Red Hat

Ansible is being used more frequently than ever, as shown in the following diagram, which shows the number of downloads of the main package for each of the tools from the Debian repository per year:

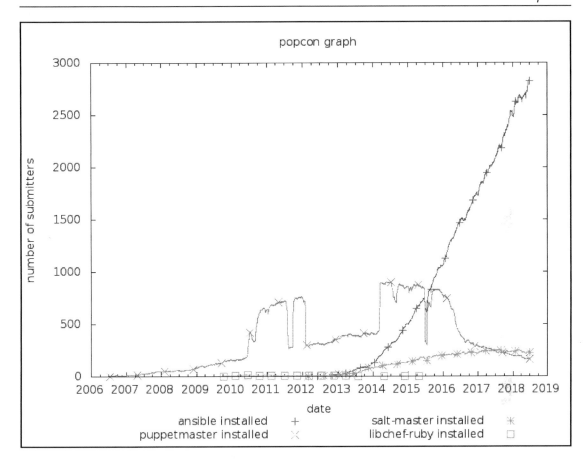

The previous figure was an Ansible, Puppet, Chef, and SaltStack Popularity contest statistics on the Debian repository. It was generated using the following link `https://qa.debian.org/popcon-graph.php?packages=ansible%2C+puppetmaster%2C+salt-master%2C+libchef-rubyshow_installed=onwant_legend=onwant_ticks=onfrom_date=2010to_date=2018hlght_date=date_fmt=%25Y-%25mbeenhere=1`. This link can be used to generate time graphs about other Debian packages through time.

Ansible: simple, lightweight, and powerful

Ansible is a leading orchestration platform that allows for automation, host configuration management, and the deployment of applications and virtual machines. Ansible can automate a range of IT infrastructure features, from simple, daily, and repetitive tasks to machine provisioning or the continuous integration and deployment of DevOps applications. It is very flexible and can cover bare-metal machines, virtual machines and platforms, and public or private cloud environments. Ansible can also manage network devices from switches, routers, and firewalls. It can also cover the setup of applications, the configuration and behavior of database management systems, package managers, and simple user applications:

Ansible logo

If this is your first book about configuration management and you are looking for an easy and simple method to follow, you are in the right place.

One command is enough to install Ansible on Linux using the system's package manager from the distribution repository. Another way is to use Python's PyPI package manager for a faster and simpler installation. After that, it can simply be used in a similar way to execute any command. We would recommend going an extra step for a more complex or larger environment by editing the Ansible configuration file, so that it reads `/etc/ansible/ansible.conf`, filling in the inventory, and adding some group variables. Ansible does not require an agent installation on the client, but with a few extra steps, the connection can be made more secure. Ansible uses YAML, a simple configuration management language for Ansible playbooks, which is a human-readable coding language, so scripts can be written without much difficulty. When sending commands for specific tasks, the Ansible server translates the YAML code to the actual configuration code to the clients for immediate execution.

For most of the tutorials in this book, Debian-based systems will be used for the servers and Linux clients. The location and package names of the configuration files may vary between distributions.

The Ansible host server is the only machine where recommended computing resources are to be met in order to run the engine correctly. As it is agentless, the clients only receive tasks in the form of commands that get executed on the system directly. Some Ansible modules may consume a fair amount of the network traffic by sending data from one machine to another. This is the lowest amount of traffic required to carry out a task, since Ansible only uses a tiny portion of traffic to submit the command to the hosts.

The rapid growth of Ansible has made it a very powerful tool. It is now considered the leading automation engine in the market. With its huge community support (Ansible Galaxy and GitHub projects) and Red Hat's proprietary management add-ons (Ansible Tower), its users have a wide variety of roles, modules, and add-ons to choose from that can automate every conceivable IT task.

Ansible offers its users the following features:

- Systems configuration management
- Agile application deployment following the best DevOps practices
- Simplified orchestration and automation
- Zero-downtime, continuous deployment
- Support for cloud-native applications
- Simple and optimized container adoption
- Embedded security and compliance policy in automated tasks
- Streamlined host provisioning
- Support for multi-tier deployment
- Support for heterogenic IT infrastructures
- Support for multi-layered computer architecture
- Support for **infrastructure-as-a-service (IaaS)** deployment
- Support for **platform-as-a-service (PaaS)** deployment
- Support for scalability for a fast-growing environment
- Support for push and pull models for task execution
- Fast host fact-sharing between servers for better redundancy and performance
- Configuration for a variety of network devices
- Management and monitoring of storage devices
- Control of database management systems

The Ansible module updates that come with each new release are a very good indication of the technologies and features that are officially supported. The modules allow the user to write simpler playbooks to perform more complex tasks.

Ansible orchestration and automation

With the rapid growth of IT infrastructures and a shift in the way applications are being deployed, IT administrators' tasks have grown in scale and complexity. Ansible seamlessly merges orchestration and configuration management in a very handy platform that allows IT administrators to define a selected number of nodes, applications, and network devices to be configured in a desired state by making clear which actions should be taken to remove repetition and reduce complexity. Ansible can be used in a variety of ways, which we will cover in the next section.

Orchestration

As well as configuration management, Ansible also offers high-end orchestration. This makes the organization and management of the interactions between multiple configuration tasks well-structured. It simplifies and orders complex and chaotic configuration management and administration tasks. According to the status of the infrastructure, and the users' demands, applications, and data-versioned behaviors, Ansible orchestration will generally bring the infrastructure back to the desired state by configuring the appropriate services and policies via the CM tool into the failed component and make it work properly.

IT orchestration can get very complex when dealing with DevOps class tasks, such as the **continuous integration and deployment (CI/CD)** of applications or **infrastructure as a code (IaC)**. Ansible is capable of converting those tasks to automated workflows that run a number of playbooks in a well-defined structure, featuring all sorts of Ansible pre-defined modules, plugins, and APIs to communicate, execute commands, and report facts from any number of hosts, devices, and services.

Automate everything

Ansible is the path to take for better infrastructure automation, application deployment, and provisioning. It is the open source approach to an automated and modernized IT environment. Ansible is the key to enabling IT administrators to automate their daily tasks, freeing up their time to allow them to focus on delivering quality services. This not only impacts the IT department, but the business as a whole. The following diagram shows the reach of Ansible's multiple functionalities:

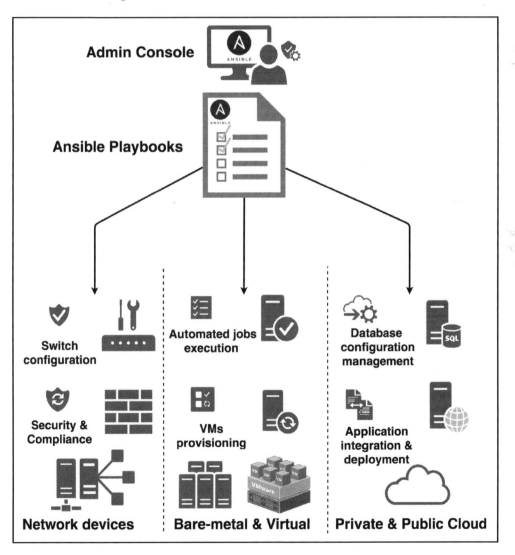

Provisioning

Instance provisioning using Ansible covers the configuration and setup of bare-metal machines and servers. It relies on its predefined APIs to create and configure the local virtualized infrastructure. It can also manage hybrid, private, and public cloud instances, resources, and applications. Ansible can automatically install and configure an application and its libraries. It uses OS bootstrap and a kickstart script to initiate bare-metal machine provisioning using very simple playbooks and built-in modules. Using the same simple playbooks and different modules, Ansible can also provision instances, networking, and VMs in a public, private, or hybrid cloud very easily.

Configuration management

Using the power of playbooks and inventory, IT administrators can use Ansible to execute an update, patch, or configuration modification on a number of hosts, network devices, and applications. Playbooks describe the infrastructure in both simple, human-readable terms for other people to use, and machine-parsable code that can be used on any machine running Ansible. The execution of an Ansible configuration is state-driven, which means that it does not need to check the system or service state to know how to adapt in order to increase the task's reliability.

Application deployment

When we talk about applications that are managed by Ansible, we are talking about full life cycle control. Any users who have access to the Ansible server node, from IT administrators to application developers and project managers, will be able to manage all aspects of the application. Ansible takes the application package, deploys it to all the production servers, sets it up, and configures and initiates it. It can even test the package and report its status. This feature covers multi-tier applications, allowing zero-downtime rolling for a seamless application update.

Continuous delivery and continuous integration

Ansible ensures a stable environment for both developers and IT administrators for the continuous delivery and integration of applications. Automating as much as possible of the application turnaround means it is quick and unnoticeable to the application users. Ansible automation and orchestration is multi-tier and multi-step, which allows for finer control over operations and hosts. We can write Playbooks to manage the continuous integration and delivery of applications while ensuring the desired state of various components, such as load balancers and several server nodes.

Ansible project and Ansible Tower

After being bought by Red Hat, Ansible continued to offer a free open source platform, which is currently called the Ansible Project. Red Hat has created proprietary management add-ons that offer an advanced control and centralization of the infrastructure, called Ansible Tower. Red Hat runs the Ansible Automation platform, which is composed of the Ansible Engine and Ansible Tower. This product is fully supported by Red Hat as one of its lead projects.

Ansible project

The Ansible project is a build-up of functionalities that come from the original company, AnsibleWorks. It is a community-built automation engine. It is free, open source, and available for anyone to download or install on any Linux OS, using the package manager, source compiling, or Python PyPI. It is very simple, powerful, and agentless.

To use the Ansible automation engine, users do not need any third-party applications or interfaces. They can simply send a command or write a playbook and execute it directly to the engine. This allows the user to access a variety of predefined modules, plugins, and APIs working as building blocks for managing all kinds of IT tasks and network objects. As it is agentless, Ansible relies on SSH to manage the Linux hosts, and WinRM for the Windows hosts. The SSH protocol is also used to control some of the network devices. Some more unusual devices or cloud and virtualization services require the use of Ansible pre-defined APIs to help manage or access them.

Nodes can be defined by their IP addresses or hostname; for the latter, we will have to rely on a DNS server or the local DNS file. APIs are used to communicate with third-party services, such as public or private clouds. Modules, which constitute Ansible's biggest pre-defined function library, allow the users to simplify long and complex tasks into a few lines in a playbook. They cover a large number of tasks, systems, packages, files, datastores, API calls, network device configurations, and so on. Finally, Ansible plugins are used to improve Ansible's core functionality, such as fast host caching, to avoid facts gathering on the network.

Ansible Tower

Ansible Tower is the Red Hat proprietary layer that sits on top of the Ansible project engine. It is made up of a number of add-ons and modules, composed of REST APIs and web services, that work together to create a friendly web interface that acts as an automation hub from which the IT administrator can select a number of tasks or playbooks to be executed on a number of machines. It still relies on the Ansible Engine to send commands and collect the reports. Ansible Tower cleverly collects the status of tasks and the reports that come back from hosts. All of this data is presented in the Ansible dashboard, showing hosts, the status of the inventory, and the recent jobs, activities, and snapshots:

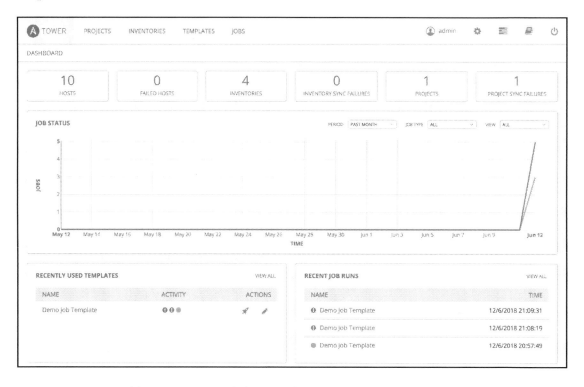

Ansible Tower can only be installed on Red Hat 7, CentOS 7, and Ubuntu 14.04/16.04 LTS.

Ansible Tower scales as the environment grows, and acts accordingly by showing in real-time all the statuses of the hosts, tasks, and playbooks. It highlights the successful playbook jobs, as well as those that failed to run, in order to troubleshoot any issues. In its multi-playbook workflows, the user can create pipelines of playbooks to be executed in sequence on any type of inventory, using one or more users' credentials and on a personalized timescale. With pipelining enabled, an IT administrator can automate complex operations (application provisioning, continuous deployment with containers, running test workflows) by breaking them down into smaller tasks using pipelines and, depending on the output (success or failure), run a specific play.

Ansible Tower offers a smart inventory platform that enables you to pull the host's inventory from any source, including a public or private cloud, or a local CMDB. The smart inventory builds hosts caching, which allows the user to run playbooks based on the facts of the hosts, which are pieces of information and properties related to them and gathered by Ansible. It also allows you to set up built-in notifications about the status of tasks, workflows, and playbooks via email, SMS, and push notifications on third-party platforms, such as Slack or Hipchat. Ansible Tower also allows task scheduling for routine updates, device patching, and custom backup schedule options. The following diagram shows the layers of the full Ansible Engine provided by Red Hat:

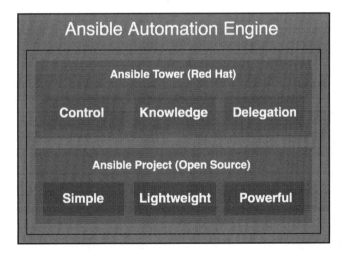

Currently, Red Hat Ansible Tower offers a 30-day trial license for a hands-on exploration and test of its features. Any user can use it to decide if their environment will benefit from it.

In this book, we will mainly focus on the open source Ansible Engine, as it is free and accessible to everyone. We believe that learning Ansible has to be started with the basic no-UI version to better understand the inner mechanics of the tool. The reader can migrate easily to Ansible Tower with the engine skills that they have already acquired.

 There are a number of open source solutions that provide some of the functionalities of Ansible Tower. The most common of these is Ansible Semaphore, which is available at `https://github.com/ansible-semaphore/semaphore`.

Summary

In this chapter, we introduced Ansible and listed its key features and the advantages that it can offer to the user when employed properly. We have also discussed the enterprise version of Ansible Tower, which is developed and supported by RedHat. In Chapter 2, *Ansible Setup and Configuration*, we are going to start the real learning. We will begin by setting up Ansible and showing the best ways of configuring it to take it for a test drive.

References

This chapter's references are as follows:

- Ansible website: `https://www.ansible.com/`
- Red Hat website: `https://www.redhat.com/en/technologies/management/ansible`
- Puppet website: `https://puppet.com/`
- Chef website: `https://www.chef.io/chef/`
- SaltStack website: `https://saltstack.com/`

2
Ansible Setup and Configuration

As Ansible is agentless, unlike other configuration management platforms, it only requires a master node installation. Ansible is also particularly light due to its lack of daemons, database reliance, and keep-on-running services.

Following our introduction to Ansible, we are now going to look at different ways of installing Ansible in your environment, such as bare-metal, in the cloud, and the use of Docker containers. We will also look at how to install Ansible on multiple Linux operating systems, both from a package manager and from the source. Finally, we will look at how to prepare and configure a host so that it is Ansible-controllable. This chapter will cover the following:

- Ansible master nodes and basic Linux installation
- Ansible container setup
- Ansible source installation
- Ansible AWS instance setup
- Ansible configuration
- Ansible configuration on Linux and Windows clients

Ansible master node installation

Ansible uses **Secure Shell (SSH)** and WinRM to manage its host clients. All installation happens on either the management node or the master node, or possibly on multiple nodes when redundancy is needed. We will proceed into the installation of Ansible from source, as with Python PyPI on two major Linux families: Debian (which includes Debian, Linux Mint, Kali Linux, Ubuntu, and Ubuntu Mate) and Red Hat (which includes Red Hat, Fedora, CentOS, and Scientific Linux). We will also be looking at the Ansible installation process for Mac OS X, Python PyPI, and how to install it from the source. We will cover cloud usage and containerized Ansible.

If you have a choice, we recommend using the default package manager for Red Hat, CentOS, Debian, Ubuntu, and Mac OS X. Using the package manager allows the installation of the latest stable version of Ansible. Python PyPI can also be relied on for its capacity to deliver the latest stable version of Ansible, especially when using an old LTS or a stable Linux version.

For use in a cloud environment, there are many community instances of Ansible. We recommend using the most popular instance with the appropriate version.

Prerequisites

In this respect, Ansible is awesome. For a Linux package installation, all you need is Python 2 (version 2.6 or higher) or Python 3 (version 3.5 or higher). For source installation, we may need the development suite, such as the `build-essential` package for the Debian family, or the `Development Tools` group package for the Red Hat family.

 Most package managers of Linux operating systems will automatically download the appropriate Python version and its dependencies when asked to install Ansible.

As for Mac OS X, having Homebrew and Xcode installed should do the job. Bear in mind that these are a requirement needed to install the Ansible package.

 Before using Ansible Mac OS X, you need to run a command as a root user to allow yourself to control more than 15 hosts. This has something to do with the limit of files to be handled simultaneously. The command is `sudo launchctl limit maxfiles unlimited`.

With regard to the Ansible container installation, we need a container engine. In our case, we will be using Docker, or any equivalent platform, such as Singularity or Shifter. For the cloud installation, all we need is an SSH client to connect to the AWS instance. Other cloud providers, such as Google Cloud Platform or Microsoft Azure, also support Ansible instances.

You can always create your own customized cloud instance on any platform. Our recommendations are for the vast majority of use cases where we believe that the AWS-supported and community instances are tested by many users, and they are as stable and reliable as they can be.

Other requirements are not mentioned here because they are not strictly essential for the Ansible main functions and modules, but instead for very specific plugins and modules. We will cover these when we talk about those modules and plugins.

Red Hat, CentOS, and Fedora package installation

If you are using Yellowdog Updater, Modified (Yum), you will have an extra step, since Ansible is not located in the default RHEL repositories. As you may have experienced when installing tools in the past, the **Extra Package for Enterprise Linux (EPEL)** is often required to be installed before you can use the package manager to install the tools. This is a very straightforward step. We first need to download the epel-release rpm file from the Fedora Project website: http://fedoraproject.org/wiki/EPEL. We then need to install it using rpm as follows:

```
sudo rpm -i epel-release-latest-7.noarch.rpm
```

Tools downloaded from EPEL are not actually tested by Red Hat quality engineers, therefore extra care should be taken when downloading on production servers it as may disrupt support.

The Ansible engine repository (available at https://access.redhat.com/articles/3174981) is another valid repository to download the latest releases from Ansible. To access its packages using Red Hat Linux only, we first need to enable it as follows:

```
sudo subsription-manager repos --enable rhel-7-server-ansible-2.5-rpms
```

After that, the package manager will need to update its cache, the package list. We use Yum to do so, as follows:

```
sudo yum update
```

Just like installing any other package using Yum, we need to specify `ansible` as the input for the `install` option:

```
sudo yum install ansible
```

Most of the Red Hat family operating systems should accept those commands to set up Ansible. Fedora 18 and later versions have a next-generation package manager, **Dandified Yum** (**DNF**). This is currently the default package manager from Fedora 22 and onwards. After installing the EPEL package using RPM, we need to run the following command to update the DNF package list:

```
sudo dnf -y update
```

We then install Ansible using the following command:

```
sudo dnf -y install ansible
```

Using the Red Hat family of operating systems, Ansible installation can be done by getting the appropriate RPM file and installing it using RPM. First, we need to download the appropriate RPM file from the Ansible releases link: `https://releases.ansible.com/ansible/rpm/`. Download the RPM file with the desired Ansible version and install it as follows:

```
sudo rpm -Uvh ansible-2.5.5-1.el7.ans.noarch.rpm
```

If needed, RPM files can also be built and installed from a source easily. We recommend using the official GitHub Ansible repository. Firstly, we need to get the project folder using Git. We may need to have Git installed already to be able to download it easily:

```
git clone https://github.com/ansible/ansible.git
cd ansible
```

Then, we need to build the Ansible `rpm` file and install it using the same command:

```
make rpm
sudo rpm -Uvh rpm-build/ansible-*.noarch.rpm
```

Debian package installation

For Debian users, as you may already know, if you want to use the latest versions of a tool, you need to be running the latest stable or testing release of the Debian OS. The testing release is not recommended, but is used by some people. Because Debian is very reliable, operating system administrators tend to set up a Debian server and then forget about it for years and years, because it continues to do what it is supposed to do without a single problem. Often, administrators tend to have lots of old, stable Debian releases running. We don't recommend using these if you want to have the latest Ansible version, with all its perks, modules, and plugins, unless you do an alternative installation (with PyPI, a source installation, or via a container).

We are going to be using Debian 9 (Stretch) as it is the latest Debian stable release. Debian 9 allows you to use many Ubuntu package sources for Ansible. We can either add the DEB line to the source.list file or add the **Personal Package Archives** (**PPA**) to the list. First, we need to install the software properties package:

```
sudo apt-get install -y software-properties-common
```

We then use a text editor and add the following DEB to /etc/apt/source.list:

```
deb http://ppa.launchpad.net/ansible/ansible/ubuntu trusty main
```

A faster way to add a DEB line at the end of the source file is as follows:
echo "deb http://ppa.launchpad.net/ansible/ansible/ubuntu trusty main" >> /etc/apt/source.list

Then authenticate the link by adding its key to apt:

```
sudo apt-key adv --keyserver keyserver.ubuntu.com --recv-keys
93C4A3FD7BB9C367
```

For the latest Debian release, the PPA repository can be used directly as well, by adding the link to the APT repository: sudo apt-add-repository ppa:ansible/ansible

Usually, adding a repository requires you to update the package manager cache:

```
sudo apt update
```

Then we can install Ansible:

```
sudo apt install -y ansible
```

Most of the tutorials in further chapters are carried out on Debian 8 (Jessie) with Ansible installed and updated using Python PyPI. This is just as stable, up to date, and reliable as any other standard way of installing Ansible on an operating system's latest release.

Ubuntu package installation

The best way to install Ansible on a recent release is to add the Ansible PPA for Ubuntu `ppa:ansible/ansible` (`launchpad.net/~ansible/+archive/ubuntu/ansible`). This should be added using the following command:

```
sudo apt-add-repository ppa:ansible/ansible
```

Adding a PPA repository requires you to confirm a key server setup. This is accepted by pressing *Enter*.

We then need to update the package manager cache, also called the system packages index, as follows:

```
sudo apt update
```

Finally, we can install Ansible:

```
sudo apt install ansible
```

macOS X package installation

Installing Ansible on the MAC OS X system can be achieved using one of two tools. The first, which uses Python PyPI, is described in the following section. The second uses the Mac OS X open source package management system Homebrew (brew.sh). In this section, we will be describing how to install Ansible using Homebrew.

To be able to use Homebrew, we first need to make sure it is installed, as it is not a default system application. You need to build it into the system using a Ruby compiler. For that, you also need to install Xcode (found here: `developer.apple.com/xcode/`) and accept its user license. We then run the following command on its Terminal:

```
/usr/bin/ruby -e "$(curl -fsSL
https://raw.githubusercontent.com/Homebrew/install/master/install)"
```

This command may take some time depending on your internet access and computer speed.

We can then use Homebrew to install Ansible:

```
brew install ansible
```

Python PyPI installation

To be able to install Ansible using PyPI, we first need to have PyPI installed. It can be easily installed using most package managers, some of which are outlined in the following section.

The Red Hat Yum installation is implemented as follows:

```
sudo yum install -y python-pip
```

The Debian APT installation uses the following command:

```
sudo apt install -y python-pip
```

For other Linux systems, using Python:

```
sudo easy_install pip
```

The Mac OS X Homebrew installation is as follows:

```
brew install python-pip
```

From the PyPI repository, by having PyPI installed:

```
sudo pip install ansible
```

We can also use a GitHub source to get the latest development version:

```
sudo pip install git+https://github.com/ansible/ansible.git@devel
```

> To choose a specific version of Ansible using PyPI, we can use the following command: `sudo pip install ansible==2.4.0`. To upgrade the latest version, we can add the `--upgrade` option so the command looks as follows: `sudo pip install ansible --upgrade`.

Source GitHub or tarball installation

Being able to build up Ansible from its source is helpful for users in an uncommon environment, or for those who have some special requirements, such as setting up Ansible without the need of a package manager or being limited to the latest stable version of Ansible. Using the development version of Ansible (or beta) always puts its user at risk of having unstable modules and plugins, but also allows for early access to future modules.

To acquire Ansible's source package, we can use two different methods: downloading the .tar file, or cloning the GitHub repository of the project. The Ansible project source files are located in its releases page (releases.ansible.com/ansible/), and the GitHub source can be cloned from the official GitHub project (github.com/ansible/ansible).

To download the tarball file, use your favorite file fetching tool (such as curl, wget, or axel):

```
wget -c https://releases.ansible.com/ansible/ansible-2.6.0rc3.tar.gz
```

We then need to un-archive the tarball:

```
tar -xzvf  ./ansible-2.6.0rc3.tar.gz
```

Alternatively, we can use Git to clone the GitHub project locally. We need to make sure that Git is installed on the system, and then we can start cloning. This process is shown for a number of systems in the following snippets.

The following command line shows how to install git on a Linux from the Red Hat family:

```
sudo yum install -y git
```

The following command line shows how to install git on a Linux from the Debian family:

```
sudo apt install -y git
```

The following command line shows how to install git on Mac OS X:

```
brew install git
```

On all the systems, to clone the Ansible GitHub project:

```
git clone https://github.com/ansible/ansible.git --recursive
```

We then need to start building Ansible, either by getting the tarball or the source from GitHub:

```
cd ./ansible*
```

To make sure that all the requirements for building Ansible are met easily, we will be using Python PyPI. The PyPI installation on multiple systems is covered in the preceding section. For this section, we will use `easy_install`, which only requires you to install a version of Python on the system:

```
sudo easy_install pip
```

We now install the Python requirements:

```
sudo pip install -r ./requirements.txt
```

We need to set up the environment as follows to be able to use Ansible:

```
source ./hacking/env-setup
```

Updating Ansible when using the GitHub project can be trickier. We need to pull the project and its submodules as follows:

```
git pull --rebase
git submodule update --init --recursive
```

Every time those commands are executed, we need to make sure that the environment is properly set up:

```
echo "export ANSIBLE_HOSTS=/etc/ansible/hosts" >> ~/.bashrc
echo "source ~/ansible/hacking/env-setup" >> ~/.bashrc
```

The location of the environmental source can change whenever the Ansible source is located. The Ansible inventory (usually located in `/etc/ansible/hosts`) and its configuration file (usually located in `/etc/ansible/ansible.cfg`) can also be changed to accommodate permission restrictions or provide Ansible users with easier access to enable modifications or restrict them. This will be covered in more detail later in this chapter.

Ansible Docker container installation

Using Ansible on a container requires a container engine to be running. There are multiple choices for which container to use, the most famous ones being Docker, Kubernetes, and Red Hat OpenShift. In this book, we will only cover Docker. We need to have a Docker engine running on the machine that is going to host the Ansible Container. The information about Docker installation can be found in its official documentation at: `https://docs.docker.com/install/`. This covers a large number of operating systems.

Here, we will assume that the Docker engine is installed, and that the current user has been added to the Docker group so that they can manage the local Docker containers on the machine. You can also choose to build your own container by selecting any of the systems that you are familiar with for the source image. Make sure that you have all requirements installed. The following is an example of a basic Dockerfile on Linux Alpine, one of the lightest systems used on containers:

```
FROM alpine:3.7

RUN echo "#### Setting up the environment for the build dependencies ####"
&& \
set -x && apk --update add --virtual build-dependencies \
    gcc musl-dev libffi-dev openssl-dev python-dev

RUN echo "#### Update the OS package index and tools ####" && \
    apk update && apk upgrade

RUN echo "#### Setting up the build dependecies ####" && \
   apk add --no-cache bash curl tar openssh-client \
    sshpass git python py-boto py-dateutil py-httplib2 \
    py-jinja2 py-paramiko py-pip py-yaml ca-certificates

RUN echo "#### Installing Python PyPI ####" && \
    pip install pip==9.0.3 && \
    pip install python-keyczar docker-py

RUN echo "#### Installing Ansible latest release and cleaning up ####" && \
    pip install ansible –upgrade \
    apk del build-dependencies && \
    rm -rf /var/cache/apk/*

RUN echo "#### Initializing Ansible inventory with the localhost ####" && \
    mkdir -p /etc/ansible/library /etc/ansible/roles /etc/ansible/lib
/etc/ansible/ && \
    echo "localhost" >> /etc/ansible/hosts

ENV HOME                    /home/ansible
ENV PATH                    /etc/ansible/bin:$PATH
ENV PYTHONPATH              /etc/ansible/lib
ENV ANSIBLE_ROLES_PATH      /etc/ansible/roles
ENV ANSIBLE_LIBRARY         /etc/ansible/library
ENV ANSIBLE_SSH_PIPELINING          True
ENV ANSIBLE_GATHERING               smart
ENV ANSIBLE_HOST_KEY_CHECKING       false
ENV ANSIBLE_RETRY_FILES_ENABLED     false

RUN adduser -h $HOME ansible -D \
```

```
    && chown -R ansible:ansible $HOME

RUN echo "ansible ALL=(ALL) NOPASSWD: ALL" >> /etc/sudoers \
    && chmod 0440 /etc/sudoers

WORKDIR $HOME
USER ansible

ENTRYPOINT ["ansible"]
```

We then build the container using the `build` function on Docker:

`docker build -t dockerhub-user/ansible .`

The build might take some time to finish. We can then try and run our Ansible container in several different ways, depending on how we are going to use it. For example, we can verify the Ansible version on the container:

`docker run --rm -it -v ~:/home/ansible dockerhub-user/ansible --version`

We can also run a ping task:

`docker run --rm -it -v ~:/home/ansible \`
`-v ~/.ssh/id_rsa:/ansible/.ssh/id_rsa \`
`-v ~/.ssh/id_rsa.pub:/ansible/.ssh/id_rsa.pub \`
`dockerhub-user/ansible -m ping 192.168.1.10`

By changing the ENTRYPOINT of our Dockerfile code from [ansible] to [ansible-playbook], we can create a script that can use our container to work as if docker-playbook is installed. This will be explained further in Chapter 3, *Ansible Inventory and Playbook*. Create a script called ansible-playbook and add it to the PATH environmental variable with the following code:

```
#!/bin/bash
    -v ~/.ssh/id_rsa:/ansible/.ssh/id_rsa \
    -v ~/.ssh/id_rsa.pub:/ansible/.ssh/id_rsa.pub \
    -v /var/log/ansible/ansible.log \
    dockerhub-user/ansible "$@"
```

Ensure that the script has execution permission by using the chmod +x command line. It can be copied or sym-linked to /usr/local/bin/ to automatically add it to PATH.

This script can be used as follows to execute a playbook on a specific host located in the `inventory` folder:

```
Ansibleplaybook play tasks.yml -i inventory/hosts
```

Ansible instance on AWS

There are multiple public cloud providers, such as Google Cloud Platform or Microsoft Azure, that offer the same service as **Amazon Web Services** (**AWS**). In this section, we aren't going to cover much of the installation process, since the instance is already pre-installed and configured.

Instead, this section will be a brief step-by-step guide to setting up an already existing Ansible instance on AWS. First, we need to access the EC2 Dashboard of our AWS account:

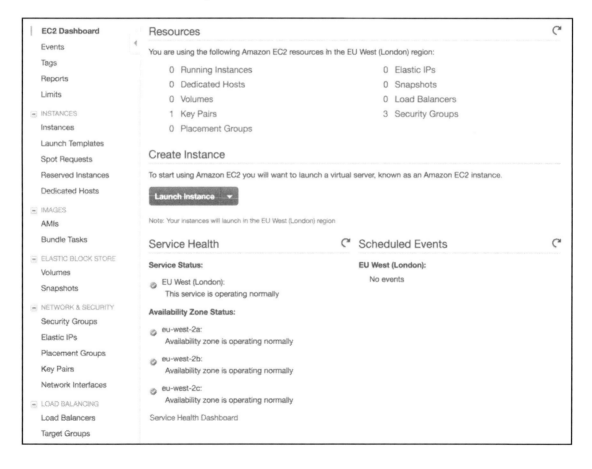

We then choose to launch a new instance and look for the `Ansiblemaster` instance. Be careful not to choose one of the Ansible Tower instances:

We then select the number of computer resources that we want to give to our instance:

Then, we add in the disk space to be used by the instance, as follows:

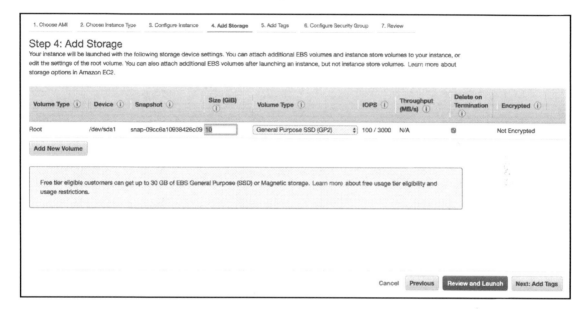

We then confirm and launch the instance:

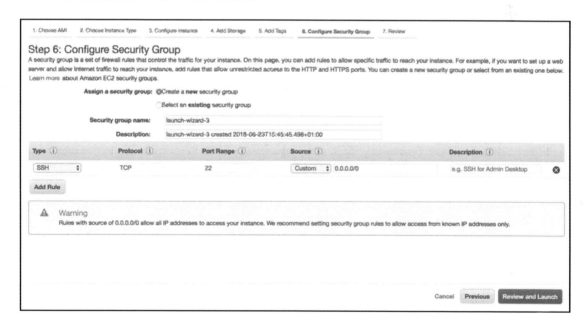

We can either create a new SSH access key or use an old one:

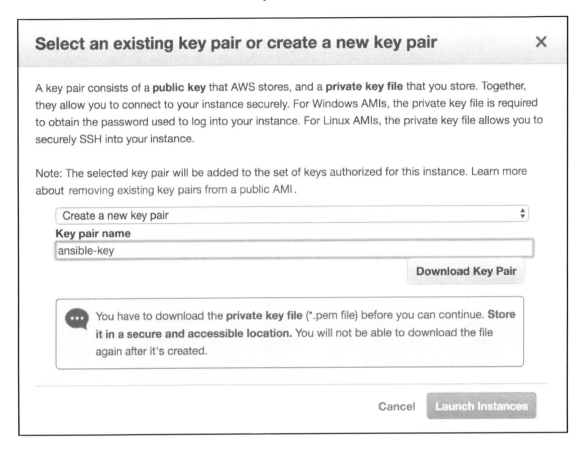

On our local terminal, we set permissions into the key file and use SSH to access the instance:

```
alibi@alibi-ml ~/Downloads> chmod 400 ansible-key.pem
alibi@alibi-ml ~/Downloads> ssh -i "ansible-key.pem" ec2-user@ec2-35-176-45-90.eu-west-2.compute.amazonaws.com
The authenticity of host 'ec2-35-176-45-90.eu-west-2.compute.amazonaws.com (35.176.45.90)' can't be established.
ECDSA key fingerprint is SHA256:YtL0yzKvOsQlYX9LJ1VxyRNwtSX+5NzRCUAgPFw/HKc.
Are you sure you want to continue connecting (yes/no)? yes
Warning: Permanently added 'ec2-35-176-45-90.eu-west-2.compute.amazonaws.com,35.176.45.90' (ECDSA) to the list of known hosts.
Last login: Sun Nov  5 07:31:30 2017 from 117.195.202.115
[ec2-user@ip-172-31-28-161 ~]$
```

We can check Ansible's version and configuration. We can always update it to the necessary or the latest stable version. The following print screens show how to move from one Ansible version to another using the instance OS package manager. First, we identify the currently installed version:

```
[ec2-user@ip-172-31-28-161 ~]$ ansible --version
ansible 2.4.1.0
  config file = /etc/ansible/ansible.cfg
  configured module search path = [u'/home/ec2-user/.ansible/plugins/modules', u'/usr/share/ansible/plugins/modules']
  ansible python module location = /usr/lib/python2.7/site-packages/ansible
  executable location = /usr/bin/ansible
  python version = 2.7.5 (default, May  3 2017, 07:55:04) [GCC 4.8.5 20150623 (Red Hat 4.8.5-14)]
[ec2-user@ip-172-31-28-161 ~]$
```

Then, we run a full system software update:

```
[ec2-user@ip-172-31-28-161 ~]$ sudo su
[root@ip-172-31-28-161 ec2-user]# yum update -y
Loaded plugins: amazon-id, rhui-lb, search-disabled-repos
epel/x86_64/metalink                                             |  31 kB  00:00:00
epel                                                            | 3.2 kB  00:00:00
rhui-REGION-client-config-server-7                             | 2.9 kB  00:00:00
rhui-REGION-rhel-server-releases                              | 3.5 kB  00:00:00
rhui-REGION-rhel-server-rh-common                             | 3.8 kB  00:00:00
(1/8): epel/x86_64/group_gz                                    |  88 kB  00:00:00
(2/8): epel/x86_64/primary                                     | 3.5 MB  00:00:00
(3/8): rhui-REGION-rhel-server-releases/7Server/x86_64/group   | 855 kB  00:00:00
(4/8): epel/x86_64/updateinfo                                  | 932 kB  00:00:00
(5/8): rhui-REGION-rhel-server-rh-common/7Server/x86_64/primary_db | 121 kB  00:00:00
(6/8): rhui-REGION-rhel-server-rh-common/7Server/x86_64/updateinfo |  33 kB  00:00:00
(7/8): rhui-REGION-rhel-server-releases/7Server/x86_64/updateinfo | 2.8 MB  00:00:00
(8/8): rhui-REGION-rhel-server-releases/7Server/x86_64/primary_db |  53 MB  00:00:01
epel                                                                    12592/12592
```

Finally, with the completion of the update process, we re-identify the Ansible version:

```
  ncurses.x86_64 0:5.9-14.20130511.el7_4              ncurses-base.noarch 0:5.9-14.20130511.el7_4
  ncurses-libs.x86_64 0:5.9-14.20130511.el7_4         nspr.x86_64 0:4.19.0-1.el7_5
  nss.x86_64 0:3.36.0-5.el7_5                          nss-softokn.x86_64 0:3.36.0-5.el7_5
  nss-softokn-freebl.x86_64 0:3.36.0-5.el7_5          nss-sysinit.x86_64 0:3.36.0-5.el7_5
  nss-tools.x86_64 0:3.36.0-5.el7_5                    nss-util.x86_64 0:3.36.0-1.el7_5
  numactl-libs.x86_64 0:2.0.9-7.el7                    openldap.x86_64 0:2.4.44-15.el7_5
  openssh.x86_64 0:7.4p1-16.el7                        openssh-clients.x86_64 0:7.4p1-16.el7
  openssh-server.x86_64 0:7.4p1-16.el7                openssl.x86_64 1:1.0.2k-12.el7
  openssl-libs.x86_64 1:1.0.2k-12.el7                  pam.x86_64 0:1.1.8-22.el7
  parted.x86_64 0:3.1-29.el7                           pciutils-libs.x86_64 0:3.5.1-3.el7
  policycoreutils.x86_64 0:2.5-22.el7                  policycoreutils-python.x86_64 0:2.5-22.el7
  polkit.x86_64 0:0.112-14.el7                         procps-ng.x86_64 0:3.3.10-17.el7_5.2
  python.x86_64 0:2.7.5-68.el7                         python-backports-ssl_match_hostname.noarch 0:3.5.0.1-1.el7
  python-dmidecode.x86_64 0:3.12.2-2.el7              python-gobject-base.x86_64 0:3.22.0-1.el7_4.1
  python-libs.x86_64 0:2.7.5-68.el7                    python-perf.x86_64 0:3.10.0-862.3.3.el7
  python-urllib3.noarch 0:1.10.2-5.el7                python2-cryptography.x86_64 0:1.7.2-2.el7
  redhat-release-server.x86_64 0:7.5-8.el7            redhat-support-tool.noarch 0:0.9.10-1.el7
  rh-amazon-rhui-client.noarch 0:2.2.141-1.el7       rhn-check.noarch 0:2.0.2-21.el7
  rhn-client-tools.noarch 0:2.0.2-21.el7             rhn-setup.noarch 0:2.0.2-21.el7
  rhnlib.noarch 0:2.5.65-7.el7                        rhnsd.x86_64 0:5.0.13-10.el7
  rpm.x86_64 0:4.11.3-32.el7                          rpm-build-libs.x86_64 0:4.11.3-32.el7
  rpm-libs.x86_64 0:4.11.3-32.el7                     rpm-python.x86_64 0:4.11.3-32.el7
  rsync.x86_64 0:3.1.2-4.el7                           rsyslog.x86_64 0:8.24.0-16.el7_5.4
  selinux-policy.noarch 0:3.13.1-192.el7_5.3         selinux-policy-targeted.noarch 0:3.13.1-192.el7_5.3
  setools-libs.x86_64 0:3.3.8-2.el7                   setup.noarch 0:2.8.71-9.el7
  shared-mime-info.x86_64 0:1.8-4.el7                subscription-manager.x86_64 0:1.20.11-1.el7_5
  sudo.x86_64 0:1.8.19p2-13.el7                       systemd.x86_64 0:219-57.el7
  systemd-libs.x86_64 0:219-57.el7                    systemd-sysv.x86_64 0:219-57.el7
  tar.x86_64 2:1.26-34.el7                            teamd.x86_64 0:1.27-4.el7
  tuned.noarch 0:2.9.0-1.el7                           tzdata.noarch 0:2018e-3.el7
  util-linux.x86_64 0:2.23.2-52.el7                  vim-minimal.x86_64 2:7.4.160-4.el7
  virt-what.x86_64 0:1.18-4.el7                        wpa_supplicant.x86_64 1:2.6-9.el7
  xfsprogs.x86_64 0:4.5.0-15.el7                       yum.noarch 0:3.4.3-158.el7
  yum-rhn-plugin.noarch 0:2.0.1-10.el7               yum-utils.noarch 0:1.1.31-45.el7

Replaced:
  grub2.x86_64 1:2.02-0.64.el7             grub2-tools.x86_64 1:2.02-0.64.el7    python-rhsm.x86_64 0:1.19.9-1.el7
  python-rhsm-certificates.x86_64 0:1.19.9-1.el7

Complete!
[root@ip-172-31-28-161 ec2-user]# ansible --version
ansible 2.5.5
  config file = /etc/ansible/ansible.cfg
  configured module search path = [u'/root/.ansible/plugins/modules', u'/usr/share/ansible/plugins/modules']
  ansible python module location = /usr/lib/python2.7/site-packages/ansible
  executable location = /bin/ansible
  python version = 2.7.5 (default, Feb 20 2018, 09:19:12) [GCC 4.8.5 20150623 (Red Hat 4.8.5-28)]
```

Finally, we can use the newly installed Ansible to orchestrate the task within our AWS environment.

Master node essential configuration

The Ansible configuration is mainly stored in the `ansible.cfg` configuration file, which is usually located in `/etc/ansible/ansible.cfg` in most system package managers and the Python PyPI installation. It may also be located in the home directory of the user who installed Ansible, or whichever location the `ANSIBLE_CONFIG` environment variable is pointing to. In this section, we will be covering the most useful configuration that can be altered using Ansible to make your life easier.

Open your `ansible.cfg` file using your favorite text editor, either in CLI mode (using vi or nano) or with a GUI (using Gedit or Atom):

```
sudo nano /etc/ansible/ansible.cfg
```

 There is no need to worry about which text editor you are using—there will always be someone who disagrees with you. Use whichever one you are most comfortable with.

Many would agree that the default configuration of Ansible is fine for normal usage. Ansible is available to use as soon as it is installed.

 From Ansible version 2.4 onwards, there is a command line, `ansible-config`, that allows the users to list the enabled options and their values to check its configuration faster.

 The disabled configuration options are implemented either by using a hash sign, #, or a semicolon, ;. The semicolon, ;, is often used to introduce an enabled option.

You can always access the Ansible example configuration file to have a look at how the options are being used. The example can be found at the following link: `raw.githubusercontent.com/ansible/ansible/devel/examples/ansible.cfg`.

Ansible's configuration file is divided into several sections. The main section that we will concentrate on is the [defaults] general section. We will start by introducing the basic parameters in this section.

- inventory: This is a parameter to indicate the file that is hosting the inventory for Ansible. On most systems, it points to /etc/ansible/hosts, as follows:

inventory = /etc/ansible/hosts

- roles_path: This is a parameter to indicate where the Ansible playbook should look for additional roles to the system default:

roles_path = /etc/ansible/roles

- log_path: This a parameter to indicate where Ansible should be storing its log. Make sure that the user running Ansible has permission to write on the specified location. An example is as follows:

log_path = /var/log/ansible.log

- retry_files_enabled: This is a parameter to enable the retry feature, allowing Ansible to create a .retry file whenever a playbook fails. It is better to keep this disabled unless you really need it. This is because it creates multiple files and clogs your playbook folder with old failed tasks that are already logged in both the Ansible log and the dashboard's playbook execution status section. Here is an example of the parameter disabled:

retry_files_enabled = False

- host_keychecking: This is a parameter that changes its recommended value depending on the environment. Usually, it is used in a continuously changing environment, where old machines get deleted and new machines take their places. It is more frequently used in a cloud or a virtualized environment, where virtual machines and deployment instances take the IP addresses of older machines. Ansible holds a key for those machines to prevent security issues. Disabling this parameter will make Ansible ignore the error messages related to the known_hosts keys:

host_key_checking = False

- `forks`: This is a parameter to define the number of parallel tasks executed to the client hosts. The default number is five, to save on both resources and network bandwidth. If there are enough resources and a large bandwidth to serve many hosts, it can be raised to the maximum number of hosts as follows:

```
forks = 10
```

- `sudo_user` and `ask_sudo_pass`: These are both legacy parameters. It is still possible to use them with the current version of Ansible, but they are not reliable. It is recommended to set these parameters when creating groups in Ansible's inventory—this is explained in more detail in the next chapter, but an example is as follows:

```
sudo_user = install
ask_sudo_pass = True
```

- `remote_port`: This is a parameter to indicate which port is to be used by SSH on the client hosts. It is also a parameter that is better set in the inventory groups:

```
remote_port = 22
```

- `nocolor`: This is an optional parameter. It allows you to show different colors for the Ansible tasks and playbook to indicate errors and successes:

```
nocolor = 0
```

The following parameters relate to the SSH connection with the host `[ssh_connection]`.

`pipelining`: This parameter enables the feature of reducing the number of SSH operations required to execute a module. This happens by executing Ansible modules without an actual file transfer and can improve Ansible's performance greatly. It requires having requiretty disabled in `/etc/sudoers` on all the managed hosts. An example of its use is as follows:

```
pipelining = True
```

The `scp_if_ssh` and `transfer_method` parameters: Both of these are responsible for file transfers between the master node and the client hosts. Choosing the `smart` value allows Ansible to choose between SFTP and SCP to opt for the most suitable protocol when transferring files:

```
scp_if_ssh = smart
transfer_method = smart
```

The following two examples relate to the persistence of the SSH connection, [persistent_connection]. We are only covering timeout for a connection and a retry for a failed one. The SSH timeout can be set by editing the value of those two parameters as follows, firstly:

```
connect_timeout = 30
```

And secondly:

```
connect_retry_timeout = 15
```

Finally, let's look at the [colors] color selection. This section gets activated when enabling the color feature in the [default] section. It allows you to choose different colors for various output statuses. This may be helpful when using a special display or to help with color blindness:

```
warn = bright purple
error = red
debug = dark gray
ok = green
changed = yellow
skip = cyan
```

On another note, we should never forget that Ansible relies on SSH to communicate with its clients. Configuration should be done on the master node to create an SSH key that is then copied to all the client hosts to enable passwordless remote access. This helps to remove passwords saved as plain text and enables full automation of the tasks. Creating an SSH key can either be simple or more complicated and more secure. We will go with the simple option:

```
ssh-keygen -t rsa
```

Keep on pressing enter while accepting the key and leaving the passphrase empty:

```
ssh-copyid user@host1
```

This task can be a bit dull and very manual. Scripting using the expect command can be very handy when trying to sort out SSH keys and authentication. First, we need to make sure that expect is installed, since it is not usually installed by default. The following examples show this process for a variety of operating systems.

This command line shows how to install the tool Expect on a Linux from the Red Hat family:

```
sudo yum install -y expect-devel
```

This command line shows how to install the tool Expect on a Linux from the Debian family:

```
sudo apt install -y expect
```

This command line shows how to install the tool Expect on MAC OS X:

```
brew install expect
```

We can then create a script file with the following:

```
#!/usr/bin/expect -f
set login "install"
set addr [lindex $argv 0]
set pw [lindex $argv 1]
spawn ssh-copy-id $login@$addr
expect "*yes/no*" {
    send "yes\r"
    expect "*?assword*" { send "$pw\r" }
    } "*?asswor*" { send "$pw\r" }
interact
```

This script should have execution privileges to be executed. It can then be used with another loop script to be executed on several machines whose IP address range or hostnames are known:

```
#!/bin/bash
password=`cat /root/installpassword.txt`
for j in 10 11 12 13 14 15 16 17 18 19 20
do
    ./expectscript 192.168.1.$j $password
done
```

Alternatively, we can use an orchestration tool to do the same task. Let's use Ansible to help with client configuration by using the simple `copy` and `shell` modules:

```
ansible all -m copy -a "src=~ /.ssh/id_rsa.pub dest=/tmp/id_rsa.pub" --ask-
pass -c install
ansible all -m shell -a "cat /tmp/id_rsa.pub >>
/home/install/.ssh/authorized_keys" --ask-pass -c install
```

 The user `install` can be a special user created on all client hosts to allow easy SSH remote access using Ansible. More details about how to set up this user can be found in the following title.

Linux client node configuration

The only important tool that is required to be installed and running on the client machine is the OpenSSH-server. All new releases of Linux use SSH as the main remote access method by default.

To make sure that everything is in place, the SSH service should always be running and the system's firewall should allow a port for SSH to service through. By default, this is port 22. This can be changed, however, and this change should be also noted in the host Ansible inventory.

For Linux clients, any extra configuration for Ansible management is more aimed at following best practice guidelines than being strictly necessary. Extra configuration can be a way to make sure that the remote clients managed by Ansible are fully automated, securely accessible, and do not require an admin intervention when running automated tasks.

 The following configuration is optional—you can choose what suits you. Add the configurations that you think will be useful and ignore the others.

Ansible can remotely manage a system using any privileged user when their credentials are at hand. However, mixing normal users, users with remote access, and management users can be messy. If a user is performing a task at the same time as Ansible is sending a task, traceback can be tricky. We recommend adding a new system user who has the sole purpose of being used by Ansible to control the host. We give this user superuser privileges and make their access passwordless to further enhance automation. This user can be the same on all the hosts of a certain inventory group to be configured at the inventory group level.

You can also create a shared folder via NFS and SMB between the hosts and the Ansible server to reduce the load when transferring data to the hosts. This task makes the hosts take the job of copying the data from the mounted shared folder, while Ansible takes care of other tasks, especially when the value of the forks is set to a high number.

Windows client node configuration

As well as Linux hosts, Ansible is capable of remotely managing Microsoft Windows hosts. This includes Windows Desktop 7, 8, and 10, and Windows Server 2008, 2008 R2, 2012, 2012 R2, and 2016.

The Windows clients require you to have some specific versions of the following applications installed:

- PowerShell 3.0 or higher
- .NET 4.0

Those two requirements are met on most Windows releases, except for Window 7 and Windows server 2008.

There is an Ansible-made PowerShell script that can carry out an automatic installation of the missing requirements that can be found at the following link: https://github.com/ PacktPublishing/Ansible-QuickStart-Guide/blob/master/Chapter2/Upgrade_ Powershell.ps1.

To be able to execute this script, or any other third-party script, we need to change the execution policy from restricted to unrestricted, run our script, and then turn the policy back to restricted. Using Windows PowerShell, run the following using local or domain administrator credentials:

```
$link =
"https://raw.githubusercontent.com/jborean93/ansible-windows/master/scripts
/Upgrade-PowerShell.ps1"
$script = "$env:temp\Upgrade-PowerShell.ps1"
$username = "Admin"
$password = "secure_password"

(New-Object -TypeName System.Net.WebClient).DownloadFile($link, $script)
Set-ExecutionPolicy -ExecutionPolicy Unrestricted -Force

&$script -Version 5.1 -Username $username -Password $password -Verbose

Set-ExecutionPolicy -ExecutionPolicy Restricted -Force

$reg_winlogon_path = "HKLM:\Software\Microsoft\Windows
NT\CurrentVersion\Winlogon"
Set-ItemProperty -Path $reg_winlogon_path -Name AutoAdminLogon -Value 0
Remove-ItemProperty -Path $reg_winlogon_path -Name DefaultUserName -
ErrorAction SilentlyContinue
Remove-ItemProperty -Path $reg_winlogon_path -Name DefaultPassword -
ErrorAction SilentlyContinue
```

Then, on all the Windows systems, a second script is essential to configure WinRM to be active and listen to Ansible commands. This script can be downloaded from the following link: https://github.com/PacktPublishing/Ansible-QuickStart-Guide/blob/master/ Chapter2/ConfigureRemotingForAnsible.ps1.

Similarly, this script also requires privileged access and the execution policy should be unrestricted. Run the following code:

```
$link =
"https://raw.githubusercontent.com/ansible/ansible/devel/examples/scripts/C
onfigureRemotingForAnsible.ps1"
$script = "$env:temp\ConfigureRemotingForAnsible.ps1"

(New-Object -TypeName System.Net.WebClient).DownloadFile($link, $script)

powershell.exe -ExecutionPolicy ByPass -File $script
```

If no errors appear, Ansible should now be able to manage these machines.

The same applies for the Windows hosts. We may need to create a local or domain administrator that is only used by Ansible to execute commands freely. Its credentials can be configured in the host inventory group as well. This can be secured using Ansible Vault to prevent having passwords written in plain text.

Summary

In this chapter, we looked at how to prepare the environment for multiple systems in order to be able to install Ansible. We also considered which configuration options were most useful in either Linux or Windows. Now that we've learned how to set up and configure Ansible, we're ready to start learning about its functional features. In the following chapter, we will be covering Ansible playbooks and inventory to better understand how orchestration works.

References

- Ansible documentation: https://docs.ansible.com/

3
Ansible Inventory and Playbook

Now that we have Ansible installed, we can move on to the next milestone. We are now going to explore two major features: Ansible inventory, for client host organization, and Ansible playbooks, to demonstrate how to write Ansible play scripts. These two functionalities combined are the foundation for Ansible's automation and orchestration. This chapter will cover how to use Ansible for quick commands or modules. We will also look at how to use its inventory to identify and configure hosts' access and group them either statically or dynamically. Finally, we will introduce Ansible playbook and look at its actions, its handler, and its variables. We will cover the following topics:

- Using simple Ansible commands with manually set hosts
- Setting up our first Ansible static inventory
- Setting up and configuring a group inventory
- Setting up and configuring a dynamic inventory
- Ansible playbook overview and usage
- Ansible playbook best practices
- Advanced Ansible playbook features

Basic Ad hoc commands on Ansible

When automating or orchestrating tasks, Ansible is mainly used with playbooks to allow subtasks to be scripted and organized in a handy pipeline. However, Ansible also has various ad hoc commands. These allow the execution of a module on a host, or group of hosts, no matter how they are identified.

Once Ansible is installed, the ad hoc command line can be used directly. It can be easily tested, either by using it with the raw module or with some simple modules, such as `ping` or `shell`. As a quick example, each Ansible instance can ping itself using the following command:

```
ansible localhost -m ping
```

We should see the following output:

```
alibi@alibi-ml ~> ansible localhost -m ping
localhost | SUCCESS => {
    "changed": false,
    "ping": "pong"
}
```

 The -m option indicates the module name that will be used while the task is running.

Some could question the Ansible ad hoc commands usefulness. They are actually a great way to test your tasks in depth, thereby making it easier to debug step-by-step smaller bits of a bigger task and capture the error location or troubleshoot slow requests. For beginners, running simple commands may help to master the basic operation of the tool by solving simpler tasks and going up a notch until you reach more complex tasks—it's better to learn how to walk before you start running.

The most common use for Ansible ad hoc commands is to run raw commands. A raw command is basically any line of Bash or PowerShell code to be sent to the host or hosts as is:

```
ansible localhost -a "echo 'Hello automated World'"
```

Something like the following output will appear after executing the command:

```
alibi@alibi-ml ~> ansible localhost -a "echo 'Hello Automated World'"
localhost | SUCCESS | rc=0 >>
Hello Automated World
```

Let's try to run a command on a different host. For this, we need the host's IP address or a fully qualified hostname, and a user where we can copy the SSH key. This can be done by physically copying the key to the user's ~/.ssh folder, or it can be done using the ssh-copyid command mentioned in Chapter 2, *Ansible Setup and Configuration*. After that, we run the following raw command to get information about the host:

```
ansible 192.168.10.10 -a "uname -a" -u setup
```

This ad hoc command will produce an output as follows:

```
alibi@alibi-ml ~/vagrant-ansible-lab> ansible 192.168.10.10 -a "uname -a" -u setup
192.168.10.10 | SUCCESS | rc=0 >>
Linux node0 4.4.0-128-generic #154-Ubuntu SMP Fri May 25 14:15:18 UTC 2018 x86_64 x86_64 x86_64 GNU/Linux
```

Alternatively, we can try and make the host perform an elevated task that requires superuser privileges:

```
ansible 192.168.10.10 -a "apt update" -u setup --become
```

This is what the output should look like when executing the preceding command:

```
alibi@alibi-ml ~/vagrant-ansible-lab> ansible 192.168.10.10 -a "apt update" -u setup --become
192.168.10.10 | SUCCESS | rc=0 >>
Hit:1 http://archive.ubuntu.com/ubuntu xenial InRelease
Get:2 http://archive.ubuntu.com/ubuntu xenial-updates InRelease [109 kB]
Get:3 http://archive.ubuntu.com/ubuntu xenial-backports InRelease [107 kB]
Get:4 http://security.ubuntu.com/ubuntu xenial-security InRelease [107 kB]
Get:5 http://archive.ubuntu.com/ubuntu xenial-updates/main Sources [310 kB]
Get:6 http://archive.ubuntu.com/ubuntu xenial-updates/universe Sources [206 kB]
Get:7 http://archive.ubuntu.com/ubuntu xenial-updates/main amd64 Packages [796 kB]
Get:8 http://archive.ubuntu.com/ubuntu xenial-updates/universe amd64 Packages [640 kB]
Get:9 http://archive.ubuntu.com/ubuntu xenial-updates/universe Translation-en [257 kB]
Fetched 2,532 kB in 0s (2,867 kB/s)
Reading package lists...
Building dependency tree...
Reading state information...
3 packages can be upgraded. Run 'apt list --upgradable' to see them.
WARNING: apt does not have a stable CLI interface. Use with caution in scripts.
```

If we use this command without the `--become` option, it will fail with a `permission denied` error message:

```
alibi@alibi-ml ~/vagrant-ansible-lab> ansible 192.168.10.10 -a "apt update" -u setup
192.168.10.10 | FAILED | rc=100 >>
Reading package lists...
WARNING: apt does not have a stable CLI interface. Use with caution in scripts.

W: chmod 0700 of directory /var/lib/apt/lists/partial failed - SetupAPTPartialDirectory (1: Operation not permitted)
E: Could not open lock file /var/lib/apt/lists/lock - open (13: Permission denied)
E: Unable to lock directory /var/lib/apt/lists/
W: Problem unlinking the file /var/cache/apt/pkgcache.bin - RemoveCaches (13: Permission denied)
W: Problem unlinking the file /var/cache/apt/srcpkgcache.bin - RemoveCaches (13: Permission denied)non-zero return code
```

This same task can be performed using Ansible modules. To do so, we use the -m option, followed by the name of the module and its arguments after the -a option, as shown in the following example:

```
ansible 192.168.10.10 -m apt -a "update_cache=yes" -u setup --become
```

Ansible also allows you to run tasks as another user by using the --become option to elevate the current user to a superuser, then selecting which user to use to run the command. It can also be done using the -e option and defining the variables in its input. The two commands are as follows:

```
ansible 192.168.10.10 -a "whoami" -u setup --become --become-user user1
ansible 192.168.10.10 -a "whoami" -u setup -e "ansible_user=user1
become=true"
```

This is what the output should look like when executing the preceding playbook:

```
alibi@alibi-ml ~/vagrant-ansible-lab> ansible 192.168.10.10 -m apt -a "update_cache=yes" -u setup --become
192.168.10.10 | SUCCESS => {
    "cache_update_time": 1530214785,
    "cache_updated": true,
    "changed": true
}
```

The ad hoc commands can also be used for a quick file transfer to multiple machines. We can either use a raw command, relying on scp or rsync, or we can also use the Ansible copy module. To be able to perform tasks on multiple hosts, we recommend using a quick static inventory. This can be done by adding a few lines to the /etc/ansible/hosts file or any other location that the Ansible configuration file points to. The file should look as follows:

```
[servers]
192.168.10.10
192.168.10.11
192.168.10.12
```

Grouping the three hosts under the servers name allows us to run tasks on all three hosts just by calling their group name. This is shown in the following example:

```
ansible servers -m copy -a "src=/home/user/file.txt
dest=/home/setup/file.txt" -u setup
```

Some tasks are so simple that writing a playbook to achieve them is a huge waste of time. Also, any Ansible ad hoc command can be made into a playbook—an Ansible user could always try some of the commands and verify their parameters, before adding them to the playbook pipeline or workflow. This is a great way of troubleshooting and applying a quick update or fix on the fly. The following example shows how we can restart a replicate of web servers one at a time by setting the number of forks to one (with the −f option). This applies the restart command host by host:

```
ansible servers -m service -a "name=httpd state=restarted" -u setup –become
-f 1
```

Ansible inventory

Ansible host management is simpler by far than all other configuration management and orchestration tools. It is basically a simple .ini file that contains a list of IP addresses, fully qualified hostnames, or short hostnames of the host clients. It also sometimes contains extra variables that define some aspects about the hosts. Generally, hosts are organized in groups with the name of the group put on top between two square brackets, such as [Group1].

 Adding a new host is as easy and simple as adding a new line to the host file, making sure it is in the right group and that it has the right variables needed to manage it.

In the default Ansible configuration file, the inventory file is located at /etc/ansible/hosts. It is an .ini file with simple text and a basic structure composed of sections, properties, and values. Being the default location, however, does not make it the best. In many cases, Ansible can be used by non-root users who do not have the privileges to edit files located outside their home directory. Our recommendation for such an environment is to have all Ansible configuration files located in a folder within the home directory of the user. This means that these users can alter their configuration to accommodate their needs. Other than changing the Ansible configuration file to point to a different inventory location, we can also choose an inventory file while executing either an Ansible ad hoc command or a playbook by adding the −i option, followed by the location of the inventory file:

```
sudo nano /etc/ansible/ansible.cfg
inventory = /home/user1/ansible/hosts
```

Or, we can use the following

```
ansible -m ping -i ~/ansible/hosts
```

The Ansible inventory does not just serve to arrange alike hosts; it is also much more useful when orchestrating tasks. Having several hosts that provide the same type of service (such as web servers, database controllers, or Web APIs) grouped in one group allows for a smarter and more efficient group control. A good host classification means that you can be more precise when applying fixes or optimizations to a specific service. Hosts can be part of multiple groups to allow them to answer to each task that is sent toward each specific aspect that they possess:

```
[webserver]
192.168.10.10
192.168.10.12

[mysqldb]
192.168.10.10
192.168.10.20

[fileserver]
192.168.10.11
192.168.10.20
```

There are two types of inventory in Ansible: static and dynamic. In a small to medium environment or infrastructure, a static inventory should do just fine. However, when there is a very large number of hosts, the tasks can get complicated and errors may start to arise. A dynamic inventory relies on a third-party service, such as AWS EC2, Rackspace, and OpenStack, to provide it with its inventory. There is always the possibility of scripting your way through and filling your Ansible static host inventory files, which can be handy if you know what you are doing.

When adding hosts with a similar pattern to an Ansible inventory file, we can simplify its syntax by changing the different pattern with a counter block, as in the following examples.

This is the original inventory:

```
[servers]
node0.lab.edu
node1.lab.edu
node2.lab.edu
node3.lab.edu
node4.lab.edu
```

This is the simplified inventory:

```
[servers]
Node[0:4].lab.edu
```

 This inventory syntax is not limited to numbers in specific formats. It can also be used for alphabetic enumeration, that is, [a:z] or [A:Z], or numbers with specific digits, such as [001:250]. It can be placed at any location in the hostname.

First let's talk about the Ansible static inventory. As its name implies, it is a static host organisation in a text file. By default, it is an .ini file that is very simply structured in lines with values:

```
node0.lab.edu

[lab1servers]
node1.lab.edu
node2.lab.edu

[lab2servers]
node3.lab.edu
```

Alternatively, it can be a YAML file, structured like a Python script structure:

```
all:
    hosts:
        node0.lab.edu
    children:
        lab1servers:
            hosts:
                node1.lab.edu
                node2.lab.edu
        lab2server:
            hosts:
                node3.lab.edu
```

 Most of our inventory examples will be written in the .ini file format. While the YAML format looks prettier and neater, it is easier and faster to write in .ini format.

A host inventory should be tolerant to all kinds and shapes of hosts. The Ansible inventory can accommodate these differences by introducing host and group variables. This is basically a way of defining each host or group with a certain aspect to help Ansible with its management. Host variables are very specific to the host and can only affect that host. The most commonly defined host variables are as follows:

- `ansible_user`: This value defines which user Ansible will be using to manage the host. It has the same function as the `-u` option, which is used in the ad hoc command.
- `ansible_host`: Some hosts may not be located in the DNS server, or we may want to give them different names. This variable allows us to point to the IP address of the host without checking how we choose to name it in the inventory.
- `ansible_port`: This is also known as `host1:port`. This is used when the hosts are accessible via a certain port other than the default.
- `ansible_connection`: This varies between `ssh`, the default connection; `local`, to communicate with the local machine; and `docker`, for running commands directly in Docker containers that rely on the local machine's Docker client. We will cover Ansible Docker usage in more detail in `Chapter 8`, *Ansible Advanced Features*.
- `ansible_become`: This option, when present, forces the host to execute all the commands on an elevated privilege (`sudo`).
- `ansible_become_user`: This allows Ansible to run a command as a specific user other than the remote access user.
- `ansible_ssh_pass`: This specifies the password to be used to access the host. This is not recommended, since the user's password will be written in plain text. The next option is better.
- `ansible_ssh_private_key_file`: This option specifies the location of the private SSH key to be used to access this VM. This is much more secure than writing the password in plain text.

This is a sample configuration:

```
ansibleserv ansible_connection: local fileserver
ansible_host: 192.168.10.10 ansible_port:22
node1.lab.edu ansible user: setup
ansible_ssh_private_key:/home/user/node1.key
node2.lab.edu ansible_become: yes
ansible_become_user: user1
```

Some host variables can be defined under the group flag, especially when the hosts share the same admin username or SSH key. The group-specific variables are defined in the same way as the host variable, in a very simple text format. Group variables, however, have an extra feature: they can be defined in two ways, either on the inventory file or on separate files. By default, Ansible looks for them in the /etc/ansible/group_vars/ folder.

Defining group variables in the inventory file should look like the following:

```
[labserver]
node0.lab.edu
node1.lab.edu

[labserver:vars]
ansible_connection=ssh
ansible_port=22
```

 When running a task on a single host, or a part of a group that has its variables defined, those variables will be applied to the host as if they are host variables.

Host groups can also be organized into groups using the :children suffix in .ini files and the children: entry in the YAML files. This is how it looks in an INI format:

```
[webservers]
node0.lab.edu
node1.lab.edu

[fileserver]
node2.lab.edu
node3.lab.edu

[server:children]
webservers
fileserver
```

Any variable applied to the parent group will get flattened to the hosts of each sub-group or child group. However, the variable of the sub-group overrides the parent variables:

```
[servers:vars]
ansible_user=setup
ansible_private_ssh_key=/home/user/ansible.key
```

The method recommended by Ansible is to define the group variables by storing them away from the inventory file and in the `group_vars` folder in separate YAML or JSON files. We will mainly be using the YAML format for the group variables file, as shown here:

```
/etc/ansible/group_vars/webserver
/etc/ansible/group_vars/fileserver
```

Each file will look as follows:

```
---
ansible_user=setup
ansible_private_ssh_key=/home/user/ansible.key
```

Hosts can also have their variables stored in a YAML file. By default, this is located in the `/etc/ansible/host_vars/` folder. They share the same structure as the group variable files.

> Variables defined in the playbook directory override those in the inventory directory. We will look closely at the playbook directory in the next section.

Ansible also supports importing an inventory from other third-party frameworks, such as cloud providers, LDAP servers, or Cobbler. For each of these, there is a specific import script that needs to be executed with Ansible after the `-i` option for inventory selection. This starts the communication between Ansible and the third-party API that returns the inventory list. The execution should happen after filling in an `.ini` file with the appropriate parameters of the third-party server or API.

Ansible playbook

Now things are starting to get interesting. Using Ansible playbooks, we will be able to achieve configuration management, orchestration, provisioning, and deployment. Playbook scripting uses the Ansible ad hoc commands in a more organized way, similar to the way in which shell scripting arranges shell commands to execute a task on a system, but more advanced than that. Ansible playbooks can set up and configure complex environments on bare metal, virtually, or on the cloud. It can sequence multi-tier machine roll-outs; apply systems, devices, and application patches and fixes; gather data from hosts or monitoring services; and act accordingly to send immediate actions to servers, network devices, and load balancers. All of these tasks can be delegated to other servers.

Playbooks are coded in a YAML data serialization format. This is a human-readable formatting, allowing the developer an easier sharing of their code and better organization as part of team projects. YAML is a very simple language compared to a traditional coding/scripting language.

Playbooks cannot do much on their own without their Ansible modules, which you can either get from Ansible Galaxy or build yourself. Modules will be explained in more detail in the next chapter. A playbook script runs multiple *plays*. Each one executes a number of *tasks*, which are composed of a number of modules on selected hosts from the Ansible inventory or from an external inventory, if this option is selected. These modules apply certain configuration changes, updates, or fixes to the selected hosts, depending on the nature of the module. A simple playbook running one play with one module to update the package manager cache is shown as follows:

```
nano ./playbook/apt_cache.yml
```

Then, we fill it in with the following code:

```
---
- name: playbook to update Debian Linux package cache
  hosts: servers
  tasks:
  - name: use apt to update its cache
    become: yes
    apt:
        update_cache: yes
```

YAML requires a very strict file structure when writing its files. Well-aligned action parameters are very important for the success of the playbook file.

We save the file and then run the `ansible-playbook` command as follows:

```
ansible-playbook playbooks/apt-cache.yml
```

The following output from the playbook's execution shows if the playbook's has made a change to the hosts:

```
alibi@alibi-ml ~/vagrant-ansible-lab> ansible-playbook playbooks/apt-cache.yml

PLAY [servers] ************************************************************

TASK [apt] ****************************************************************
changed: [192.168.10.10]
changed: [192.168.10.11]
changed: [192.168.10.12]

PLAY RECAP ****************************************************************
192.168.10.10          : ok=1    changed=1    unreachable=0    failed=0
192.168.10.11          : ok=1    changed=1    unreachable=0    failed=0
192.168.10.12          : ok=1    changed=1    unreachable=0    failed=0
```

As you can see, a task called gathering facts has been executed within our simple playbook. This is a task that runs the module setup, which collects all of the useful information about the host or hosts in question.

 When not needed, disabling the *gathering facts* task can increase the performance of your playbooks. This can be done by adding `gather_facts: False` when defining a play.

Let's try to break down the structure of a playbook script. First, let's explain the `name` option. This is an optional parameter, but it is highly recommended. When a simple and meaningful sentence is written as input to the `name` option, it helps provide a useful description of the play for improved user communication. It is also helpful when running the playbook, in order to see which plays have finished and which are still processing. A playbook output without the use of the `name` option looks as follows:

```
---
- hosts: servers
  gather_facts: False
  tasks:
  - apt:
       update_cache: yes
    become: yes
```

When executing the preceding playbook, the output should look as follows:

```
alibi@alibi-ml ~/vagrant-ansible-lab> ansible-playbook playbooks/apt-cache.yml

PLAY [servers] ********************************************************************

TASK [apt] ***********************************************************************
changed: [192.168.10.10]
changed: [192.168.10.11]
changed: [192.168.10.12]

PLAY RECAP ***********************************************************************
192.168.10.10             : ok=1    changed=1    unreachable=0    failed=0
192.168.10.11             : ok=1    changed=1    unreachable=0    failed=0
192.168.10.12             : ok=1    changed=1    unreachable=0    failed=0
```

We then have the hosts parameter or line. This is used to point to the inventory that the play should be run on, either to specify a certain group or host, or both of these combined. At the same level within the playbook, we can fill in other parameters underneath it. Those parameters can be host or group variables, used to enforce the parameters that are configured in their inventory files. These variables can be play-specified when we define them underneath the line hosts:

```
---
- name: playbook to update Debian Linux package cache
  hosts: servers
  remote_user: setup
  become: yes
  tasks:
```

They can also be task-specific when we define them within the task:

```
---
- name: playbook to update Debian Linux package cache
  hosts: servers
  tasks:
  - name: use apt to update its cache
    apt:
        update_cache: yes
    become: yes
    become_user: setup
```

We then move to the tasks list, which is basically a list module to be executed in a series. Similarly to a playbook, each task can be named using the `name:` parameter. This is highly recommended for both documentation and to follow upon the status of tasks:

```
tasks:
    - name: use apt to update its cache
        apt: update_cache=yes
```

If a task fails, the playbook execution stops with the failure. To bypass this when running a non-critical task, we can always add the `ignore_errors: True` parameter:

```
tasks:
    - name: use apt to update its cache
      apt:
          update_cache: yes
      ignore_errors: True
```

As you have seen from the two previous examples, each task's action line can be used in two different ways: either broken down or in one line. You can choose which to use based on your needs.

Finally, handlers are a major factor in making playbooks independent and automated, with less interaction for the user. They have the capacity to recognize changes and act accordingly. They are a way of controlling the system's behaviors and running actions that respond to the needs of those behaviors:

```
tasks:
- name: use apt to update its cache
  apt:
      update_cache: yes
  become: yes
  notify: pkg_installable

handlers:
 - name: pkg_installable
   apt:
       name: htop
       state: latest
   become: yes
```

When executing the preceding playbook, the output should look as follows:

```
alibi@alibi-ml ~/vagrant-ansible-lab> ansible-playbook playbooks/apt-cache.yml

PLAY [playbook to update Debian Linux package cache] ****************************

TASK [use apt to update its cache] *********************************************
changed: [192.168.10.10]
changed: [192.168.10.11]
changed: [192.168.10.12]

RUNNING HANDLER [pkg_installable] **********************************************
changed: [192.168.10.11]
changed: [192.168.10.10]
changed: [192.168.10.12]

PLAY RECAP *********************************************************************
192.168.10.10              : ok=2    changed=2    unreachable=0    failed=0
192.168.10.11              : ok=2    changed=2    unreachable=0    failed=0
192.168.10.12              : ok=2    changed=2    unreachable=0    failed=0
```

 Handlers can also be placed before the tasks in listen mode to enable action execution whenever they are triggered by multiple tasks.

Advanced Ansible playbook scripting includes conditional and loop statements to give the developer various logic and patterns to play within their playbooks.

For example, the when parameter is a way of implementing task control with conditions. Consider the following example, which only runs application updates when it is running on the right family of Linux:

```
tasks:
- name: use apt to update all apps for Debian family
  apt:
      name: "*"
      state: latest
      update_cache: yes
  become: yes
  when: ansible_os_family == "Debian"

- name: use yum to update all apps for Red Hat family
  yum:
      name: '*'
```

```
        state: latest
    become: yes
    when: ansible_os_family == "Red Hat"
```

The `when` parameter condition is not limited to values collected from the host system but also from the task's execution status, which can be one of the following:

- Result has failed
- Result has succeeded
- Result has been skipped

There are various other ways to use the playbook conditions. We will look at these in later chapters.

The loop statement can also be used. For this, we are going to use the `loop` parameter. In some cases, when we want to apply an action on multiple entries, we use the `vars:` parameter, as shown in the following example:

```
    tasks:
    - name: use apt to install multiple apps
      apt:
          name: '{{ app }}'
          state: latest
          update_cache: yes
      vars:
          app:
          - htop
          - mc
          - nload
      become: yes
```

This can also be done using the `loop` parameter:

```
    tasks:
    - name: use apt to install multiple apps
      apt:
          name: '{{ item }}'
          state: latest
          update_cache: yes
      loop:
          - htop
          - mc
          - nload
      become: yes
```

In this chapter, we have only covered the tip of the iceberg of Ansible playbooks. There are many more advanced customizations and parameters that we cannot cover in this book. Ansible is well-known for its neat and well-maintained documentation, so we recommend you have a look at this for more information.

Summary

In this chapter, we saw how Ansible can be used to run quick and simple commands. We then looked at how Ansible manages its host inventory, which helped us to understand its playbook scripting. We discovered how playbooks are structured and how they are used to orchestrate tasks. In the next chapter, we will discover Ansible Modules and learn how they are important out of all the tasks that are executed within a playbook. We will look at both Linux and Windows system modules, some network devices, and various visualization and cloud managers.

References

- Ansible blog: https://www.ansible.com/blog
- Ansible documentation: https://docs.ansible.com/ansible/latest
- Vagrant and Ansible lab GitHub repository: https://github.com/xanmanning/vagrant-ansible-lab

4

Ansible Modules

In order to master Ansible playbooks, we need to learn about modules and how useful they can be. Ansible modules are essential components that define the actions performed by every playbook. Each module is set up to enable a task to be performed. They are designed to function smoothly with no overheads because all their dependencies and requirements are covered. Ansible modules enable the user to manage several operating systems, services, applications, databases, packages managers, virtualized infrastructure datastores, and cloud environments. In this chapter, we will cover the following:

- Overview of the use of Ansible modules
- Ansible Linux modules and their varieties
- Implementing Ansible Windows modules
- A common constructor: Ansible network modules
- The Ansible cloud modules of the big three cloud providers

Ansible modules overview

When installing Ansible, the user will also receive a very handy set of modules. This set is called a module library. It is a list of predefined functions and actions to be called when using Ansible, either via ad hoc commands or by running playbooks. An Ansible user is not limited to the predefined Ansible modules; they can easily write their own using Python and JSON scripting. The modules that come with the installation of Ansible might be referred to as task plugins or library plugins, but do not mistake these for the actual Ansible plugins, which are the scripts that allow Ansible to interact with other systems, a subject for another chapter.

The Ansible module library comes with its own machine library. Use the `ansible-doc` command followed by the name of the module to find out more about how it is used and what its output variables are:

```
ansible-doc apt
```

To list all the available modules, use the -l option:

```
ansible-doc -l
```

Using modules is very simple. You need to identify the name of the module, then input its arguments if required. Not all modules require argument input (the ping module, for example, doesn't require this) but most do. For other modules, inputting arguments is optional and might allow you to personalize the action, such as in the case of the Windows reboot module. As an example, let's look at executing modules in both ad hoc and playbook mode.

Ad hoc versus playbook: the ping module

As discussed previously, Ansible ad hoc can be used for a quick check, such as running a ping command to check if the hosts are up and running. The command should look as follows:

```
ansible servers -m ping
```

The output of the command will look similar to the following:

```
alibi@alibi-ml ~/vagrant-ansible-lab> ansible servers -m ping
node0 | SUCCESS => {
    "changed": false,
    "ping": "pong"
}
node2 | SUCCESS => {
    "changed": false,
    "ping": "pong"
}
node1 | SUCCESS => {
    "changed": false,
    "ping": "pong"
}
```

The ping module can also be used in the playbook as part of the bigger script, where the result of the ping can be piped to be the condition for another action. The playbook code is as follows:

```
---
- name: Ping module playbook usage
  hosts: servers
  gather_facts: false
  tasks:
    - name: ping the local servers
      ping:
```

The output of this code will look as follows:

```
alibi@alibi-ml ~/vagrant-ansible-lab> ansible-playbook playbooks/ping_playbook.yml

PLAY [Ping module playbook usage] **********************************************:

TASK [ping the local servers] **************************************************:
ok: [node1]
ok: [node0]
ok: [node2]

PLAY RECAP *********************************************************************:
node0                     : ok=1    changed=0    unreachable=0    failed=0
node1                     : ok=1    changed=0    unreachable=0    failed=0
node2                     : ok=1    changed=0    unreachable=0    failed=0
```

Ad hoc versus playbook: the win_reboot module

The ad hoc command can be simply executed as shown in the following two examples:

```
ansible winservers -m win_reboot

ansible win servers -m win_reboot -args="msg='Reboot initiated by remote
admin' pre_reboot_delay=5"
```

The resulting output of either command will look as follows:

```
alibi@AnsibleServ:~$ ansible windows -m win_reboot --args="msg='Reboot initiated by remote admin' pre_reboot_delay=5"
winnode1 | SUCCESS => {
    "changed": true,
    "elapsed": 178,
    "rebooted": true
}
winnode3 | SUCCESS => {
    "changed": true,
    "elapsed": 178,
    "rebooted": true
}
winnode0 | SUCCESS => {
    "changed": true,
    "elapsed": 182,
    "rebooted": true
}
```

This playbook file contains two ways of restarting hosts using the same module:

```
---
- name: Reboot Windows hosts
  hosts: winservers
  fast_gathering: false
  tasks:
    - name: restart Windows hosts with default settings
      win_reboot

    - name: restart Windows hosts with personalized
      settings
      win_reboot:
        msg: "Reboot initiated by remote admin"
        pre_reboot_delay: 5
```

The resulting playbook output will look as follows:

```
alibi@AnsibleServ:~$ ansible-playbook playbook/win_reboot_playbook.yml

PLAY [Reboot Windows hosts] *************************************************

TASK [restart Windows hosts with default settings] *************************
changed: [winnode0]
changed: [winnode1]
changed: [winnode3]

TASK [restart Windows hosts with personalized settings] *******************
changed: [winnode1]
changed: [winnode0]
changed: [winnode3]

PLAY RECAP ****************************************************************
winnode0                   : ok=2    changed=2    unreachable=0    failed=0
winnode1                   : ok=2    changed=2    unreachable=0    failed=0
winnode3                   : ok=2    changed=2    unreachable=0    failed=0
```

ad-hoc versus playbook: the copy module

The Ansible `copy` module can be used in ad hoc mode to quickly run a copy job:

```
ansible servers -m copy --args="src=./file1.txt dest=~/file1.txt"
```

The output of this command should look as follows:

```
alibi@alibi-ml ~/vagrant-ansible-lab> ansible servers -m copy --args="src=./file1.txt dest=~/file1.txt"
node1 | SUCCESS => {
    "changed": false,
    "checksum": "86378c673fa5acc9f9c99aaadc08e565be15babe",
    "dest": "/home/vagrant/file1.txt",
    "gid": 1000,
    "group": "vagrant",
    "mode": "0664",
    "owner": "vagrant",
    "path": "/home/vagrant/file1.txt",
    "size": 3249,
    "state": "file",
    "uid": 1000
}
node0 | SUCCESS => {
    "changed": false,
    "checksum": "86378c673fa5acc9f9c99aaadc08e565be15babe",
    "dest": "/home/vagrant/file1.txt",
    "gid": 1000,
    "group": "vagrant",
    "mode": "0664",
    "owner": "vagrant",
    "path": "/home/vagrant/file1.txt",
    "size": 3249,
    "state": "file",
    "uid": 1000
}
node2 | SUCCESS => {
    "changed": false,
    "checksum": "86378c673fa5acc9f9c99aaadc08e565be15babe",
    "dest": "/home/vagrant/file1.txt",
    "gid": 1000,
    "group": "vagrant",
    "mode": "0664",
    "owner": "vagrant",
    "path": "/home/vagrant/file1.txt",
    "size": 3249,
    "state": "file",
    "uid": 1000
}
```

Alternatively, this can be used in a playbook with various options for a personalized result:

```
---
- name: copy a file to hosts
  hosts: servers
  become: true
  fast_gathering: false
  tasks:
```

```
- name: copy a file to the home directory of a user
  copy:
      src: ./file1.txt
      dest: ~/file1.txt
      owner: setup
      mode: 0766
```

Ansible module return values

Return values are the key feature for monitoring and managing task execution. An administrator can determine the status of each action and run other tasks accordingly, either to fix, improve, or follow up on the bigger job. Ansible modules are fitted with a variety of return values. Each module will have the common values and some extra specific ones for the role performed by the module. These extra return values can be used for numerous functionalities. In Ansible, most return values are used as input for playbook conditions and loops. This scripting allows the pipelining of actions and tasks to achieve an automated configuration management. Ansible basically collects all the useful output data about the action performed by the module and arranges it into variables presented as return values.

 There is no need to learn all the return values of these modules; you can easily get very good documentation about each module using the `ansible-doc` command. Alternatively, consult the official Ansible documentation using `module index`.

As for the most common return values, we can identify the following:

- `stdout` or `stdout_lines`: This is the variable that contains the standard output of commands executed using an execution module such as `raw`, `command`, `shell`, or `win_shell`. The `stdout_lines` have the same value and string as `stdout` but they have a more organized output—a human-readable text divided into lines.
- `stderr` or `stderr_lines`: This has the same output source as `stdout`, but this is the error message output. If the command executed returns an error message, it will be stored in this variable. The `stderr_lines` also have the same output string as `stderr` but are more organized into lines.
- `changed`: This is the return value that indicates the status of the task or action if the task has made a change to the target host. It will contain a Boolean value of `True` or `False`.

- `failed`: This is another status update return value that indicates whether the task or action has failed or not. It is also a Boolean value that can be either `True` or `False`.
- `skipped`: This is another status return value that indicates whether the task has been skipped. This occurs when a task has been triggered by a playbook condition and the condition was not met. Like the other status return values, it is a Boolean variable.
- `rc`: This stands for **return code.** It contains the return code generated by the command that is executed by the command execution modules.
- `results`: This a value that does not exist in a task unless it has a loop in it. It should contain the list of the normal module `result` per item used to loop on.
- `invocation`: This is a value that contains the method detailing how the module was invoked.
- `backup_file`: This is a value that gets filled when a module has the specific `backup=no|yes` option. It states the location where the backup file has been created.
- `msg`: This is a value containing the message that gets generated by the module to the Ansible user.

The common values get collected during the execution of the task using a register, and then are either called for by the playbook condition functions or just printed using a debugger:

```
---
- name: Restart Linux hosts if reboot is required after updates
  hosts: servers
  gather_facts: false
  tasks:
    - name: check for updates
      become: yes
      become_method: sudo
      apt: update_cache=yes

    - name: apply updates
      become: yes
      become_method: sudo
      apt: upgrade=yes

    - name: check if reboot is required
      become: yes
      become_method: sudo
      shell: "[ -f /var/run/reboot-required ]"
      failed_when: False
      register: reboot_required
```

```
            changed_when: reboot_required.rc == 0
            notify: reboot

        handlers:
          - name: reboot
            command: shutdown -r now "Ansible triggered reboot after system
    updated"
            async: 0
            poll: 0
            ignore_errors: true
```

This playbook will have the following output:

```
alibi@alibi-ml ~/vagrant-ansible-lab> ansible-playbook playbooks/return_value_playbook.yml

PLAY [Restart Linux hosts if reboot is required after updates] ****************************

TASK [check for updates] *****************************************************************
changed: [node2]
changed: [node1]
changed: [node0]

TASK [apply updates] *********************************************************************
 [WARNING]: Could not find aptitude. Using apt-get instead.

changed: [node2]
changed: [node1]
changed: [node0]

TASK [check if reboot is required] ******************************************************
ok: [node2]
ok: [node1]
ok: [node0]

PLAY RECAP *******************************************************************************
node0                      : ok=3    changed=2    unreachable=0    failed=0
node1                      : ok=3    changed=2    unreachable=0    failed=0
node2                      : ok=3    changed=2    unreachable=0    failed=0
```

Using the debugger, we can easily specify that we want one or all of the return values to be printed. The playbook task should look as follows:

```
          - name: apply updates
            become: yes
            become_method: sudo
            apt: upgrade=yes
```

```
    register: output

- name: print system update status return value
  debug:
      var: output.changed
```

Ansible also collects some extra values to be used for internal Ansible functionalities. These values are `ansible_facts`, `exception`, `warning`, and `deprecations`. They can be added by some modules to be later removed from the register variables and collected by Ansible.

Ansible Linux modules

We will start by exploring the Linux modules. These are a selection of the most commonly used modules to manage the operating systems, packages, applications, and services running on the Linux environment. We will be covering the two big Linux families, Debian and Red Hat. In this section, we will give a brief overview of the module and its useful functionalities and features. We will also look at a sample of a playbook of one of the interesting uses of this module.

We will not be covering all of the available modules that are supported in the Ansible releases. You can find full documentation for these either by running the ansible-doc command or on the official Ansible documentation in the modules index section. In this book, we will try to cover some of the community and galaxy modules that are needed to perform some tasks.

Some modules require some specific technologies to be installed on the remote hosts. Most of those requirements are usually preinstalled as basic system utilities, while you can work around others by using another tool that can do a similar job. For example, when you are using the `apt` module, the hosts are required to have `aptitude` installed on the remote Debian. Ansible will use `apt-get` to execute the job with a warning message to the user stating the unavailability of aptitude. In case the requirements are not met, Ansible will be sure to inform the user.

Before using a new module, be sure to read its documentation carefully and check if all its requirements have been met, to be on the safe side.

Linux system modules

The following is a list of the most useful Ansible modules for managing a Linux system.

The user management module

As suggested by its name, this module is for user management on a Linux system. As an example, we will make a playbook that creates a system user named `install` to be used later to manage the remote machine. The playbook script is as follows :

```
---
- name: Linux Module running
  hosts: servers
  become: yes
  gather_facts: false
  tasks:
    - name: create a system user to be used by Ansible
      user:
        name: install
        state: present
        shell: /bin/bash
        group: sudo
        system: yes
        hidden: yes
        ssh_key_file: .ssh/id_rsa
        expires: -1
```

You can always add -v or -vvv if you want extra output when running a playbook. The following screenshot shows the output of a normal run and one with the -v option:

```
▶alibi@alibi-ml ~/vagrant-ansible-lab> ansible-playbook  playbooks/modules_playbook.yml

PLAY [Linux Module running] ***********************************************************

TASK [create a system user to be used by Ansible] *************************************
changed: [node1]
changed: [node2]
changed: [node0]

PLAY RECAP ****************************************************************************
node0                      : ok=1    changed=1    unreachable=0    failed=0
node1                      : ok=1    changed=1    unreachable=0    failed=0
node2                      : ok=1    changed=1    unreachable=0    failed=0

▶alibi@alibi-ml ~/vagrant-ansible-lab> ansible-playbook  playbooks/modules_playbook.yml  -v
Using /etc/ansible/ansible.cfg as config file

PLAY [Linux Module running] ***********************************************************

TASK [create a system user to be used by Ansible] *************************************
ok: [node1] => {"append": false, "changed": false, "comment": "", "group": 27, "home": "/home/inst
all", "move_home": false, "name": "install", "shell": "/bin/bash", "state": "present", "uid": 999}
ok: [node0] => {"append": false, "changed": false, "comment": "", "group": 27, "home": "/home/inst
all", "move_home": false, "name": "install", "shell": "/bin/bash", "state": "present", "uid": 999}
ok: [node2] => {"append": false, "changed": false, "comment": "", "group": 27, "home": "/home/inst
all", "move_home": false, "name": "install", "shell": "/bin/bash", "state": "present", "uid": 999}

PLAY RECAP ****************************************************************************
node0                      : ok=1    changed=0    unreachable=0    failed=0
node1                      : ok=1    changed=0    unreachable=0    failed=0
node2                      : ok=1    changed=0    unreachable=0    failed=0
```

The same module can also be used to remove the user, either by changing their state to absent or disabling them by changing their shell to /bin/nologin. For some clustered environments, some users shared by the systems must have the same UID to be able to run tasks via the jobs handlers. The uid option can allow a particular user to have a selection of specific UIDs when creating hosts, although this is not recommended.

The modules have many special return values, which can be collected for pipelining with other modules. The most useful modules are the following:

- home: Shows the home directory for the user

- `ssh_public_key`: Allows the key print to be put into a file for multiple purposes
- `uid`: Shows the UID of the newly created user

The group management module

The group module has the same input types as the user module, but it affects the host groups. It is a basic module used to create, modify, and delete groups. It requires three basic commands for group management to be available: `groupdadd`, `groupdell`, and `groupmod`.

It is very straightforward to use. A playbook script should look as follows:

```
- name: create a new group
  group:
    name: clustergroup
    state: present
    gid: 1040
```

The hostname module

This is another simple module that does the simple job of changing a hostname. To make this module more exciting, we will use some of the playbook features with it. This module takes one input, the new hostname, and changes the hostname of the remote host. We can use the playbook predefined variable, `{{ inventory_hostname }}`. This variable calls the hostname for the Ansible inventory and uses it with the playbook.

First, we need to change the inventory file to look as follows:

```
[servers]
server0   ansible_host=192.168.10.10
server1   ansible_host=192.168.10.11
server2   ansible_host=192.168.10.12
```

Then, we use the following playbook:

```
- name: change hostname
  hostname:
    name: "{{ inventory_hostname }}"
```

After executing the playbook, you can simply test it out using an ad hoc Ansible command:

```
ansible -m shell -a hostname servers
```

The result should look as follows:

```
alibi@alibi-ml ~/vagrant-ansible-lab> ansible -m shell -a hostname servers
server1 | SUCCESS | rc=0 >>
server1

server2 | SUCCESS | rc=0 >>
server2

server0 | SUCCESS | rc=0 >>
server0
```

The sysctl control module

This is a module to manage the `sysctl` attributes. As this module can change some of the kernel behaviours, let's make sure we keep it safe. We are going to do a configuration to make the Linux server act as a gateway. We will not be covering "IPtables" rules in depth in this section. We are going to use a generic sample configuration and try to apply it via the `sysctl` module.

The playbook to run the module should contain the following:

```
- name: enable IP forwarding on IP version 4
  sysctl:
      name: net.ipv4.ip_forward
      value: 1
     sysctrl_set: yes
     state: present
    reload: yes
```

A reload option is needed when the task is required to run `sysctl -p` after the change has been made. This task, with the right firewall rules set, will enable this host to route a packet from one network interface to the other.

The service management module

This enables Linux system service management: starting, stopping, reloading, restarting, and enabling its system boot start. As an example, we will make sure that all hosts have `ntp` (that is, **network time service**) running and enabled:

```
- name: start and enable ntp service
  service:
      name: ntp
      state: started
      enabled: yes
```

The systemd module

For more advanced service management, we can use `systemd` as an alternative to service. The `systemd` module should be able to manage services on all Linux operating systems because it has the advantage of having a status special return value containing a lot of useful service data. An example playbook of how to use it is shown here:

```
- name: start and enable ntp service using systemd
  systemd:
    name: ntp
    state: started
    enabled: yes
    masked: no
    daemon_reload: yes
  register: systemd

- debug:
    var: systemd.status.Description
```

The playbook output should look as follows:

```
alibi@alibi-ml ~/vagrant-ansible-lab> ansible-playbook  playbooks/modules_playbook.yml

PLAY [Linux Module running] *********************************************************

TASK [start and enable ntp service using systemd] **********************************
ok: [server1]
ok: [server0]
ok: [server2]

TASK [debug] ***********************************************************************
ok: [server0] => {
    "systemd.status.Description": "LSB: Start NTP daemon"
}
ok: [server1] => {
    "systemd.status.Description": "LSB: Start NTP daemon"
}
ok: [server2] => {
    "systemd.status.Description": "LSB: Start NTP daemon"
}

PLAY RECAP *************************************************************************
server0                     : ok=2    changed=0    unreachable=0    failed=0
server1                     : ok=2    changed=0    unreachable=0    failed=0
server2                     : ok=2    changed=0    unreachable=0    failed=0
```

The kernel blacklist management module

This module allows you to manage the kernel blacklist of modules and drivers, which are the drivers and libraries to be excluded from the kernel devices driver initialization on the system startup. For our sample playbook, we will perform one of the most common blacklisting actions when using Nvidia GPUs—blacklisting the nouveau driver:

```
- name: addling nouveau nvidia driver to the kernel
  blaklist
  kernel_blacklist:
      name: nouveau
      state: present
```

The cron job editing module

The `cron` module is a similar tool to the `at` command, but it provides you with more timing options for the execution of the task as the `cron` module allows you to manage both `cron.d` and `crontab`. This module allows the creation and deletion of crontab entries and the creation of environmental variables. As for the playbook example, we will create `cron` `job` that makes sure that the shared folder contents have the correct permissions:

```
- name: setup a cron job
  cron:
      name: "shared folder permission enforcer"
      hour: 0
      minute: 0
      day: *
      job: "chmod -R 777 /media/shared"
      state: present
```

This module can also be handy when working with an environmental variable, such as PATH or HOME, for a crontab entry:

```
- name: link the cron PATH variable with a new binaries location
  cron:
    name: PATH
    env: yes
    value: /usr/local/app/bin
```

The SSH authorized keys management module

This module manages an SSH authorized key of a specific user account in a Linux host. Using a playbook, we will set up a new authorized key:

```
- name: add a new authorise SSH key to the user
  install
    authorized_key:
        user: install
        state: present
        key: "{{ lookup('file', '/home/install
        /.ssh/id_rsa.pub') }}"
```

This module does support many special return values. They can be used like the others to collect key data about the hosts.

The Git usage module

This module helps to deploy a tool or configuration files from a Git repository. This module requires the `git` tool to be installed on the remote host to work properly. As a playbook, we will clone the latest version of Ansible that is available on GitHub:

```
- name: clone Ansible from github
  git:
    repo: https://github.com/ansible/ansible.git
    dest: /usr/local/ansible
    clone: yes
    update: yes
```

The execution of this playbook should look as follows:

```
>alibi@alibi-ml ~/vagrant-ansible-lab> ansible-playbook  playbooks/modules_playbook.yml -v
Using /etc/ansible/ansible.cfg as config file

PLAY [Linux Module running] *******************************************************

TASK [clone Ansible from github] **************************************************
changed: [server1] => {"after": "27b4d7ed31b6688253fc4089b7a6b97f2d548167", "before": null, "chang
ed": true}
changed: [server2] => {"after": "27b4d7ed31b6688253fc4089b7a6b97f2d548167", "before": null, "chang
ed": true}
changed: [server0] => {"after": "27b4d7ed31b6688253fc4089b7a6b97f2d548167", "before": null, "chang
ed": true}

PLAY RECAP ************************************************************************
server0                    : ok=1    changed=1    unreachable=0    failed=0
server1                    : ok=1    changed=1    unreachable=0    failed=0
server2                    : ok=1    changed=1    unreachable=0    failed=0
```

The `git` module does support some special return values that help you to monitor the status of the project.

The SELinux control module

On the Red Hat environment, SELinux can be a pain to manage on one machine, let alone on a series of hosts. This Ansible module helps its user with the configuration of the SELinux mode and policy.

This module, along with some others, may require a reboot after performing the task. Ansible will always let the user know if this is the case. Some advanced modules may have an integrated option that initiates a reboot automatically if the host needs it.

As a quick playbook sample, we will ask Ansible to make SELinux permissive:

```
- name: change SELinux to permissive
  selinux:
    policy: targeted
    state: permissive
```

This module requires the `libselinux-python` library to be installed on the remote hosts to work properly. This module also has its own special return values that can be used as input for handlers or other related modules.

Linux commands modules

In this section, we are going to address the tasks that have particularly complicated Linux commands, or where we don't want to search for a module, or where you want to use your own technique. Ansible offers a list of command execution modules to help you send a command to the remote hosts. The way you want to manage your environment is up to you; Ansible is just a tool to make your work more efficient.

Running the raw command module

Compared to the other command modules, this module is the simplest in command line delivery. It basically sends the command as it is via SSH on remote hosts with no headers or options. It does not support pipelining or handlers, but it works when sending PowerShell commands to a Windows host that is configured to be managed by Ansible.

Fact gathering should be disabled when using the `raw` module to bootstrap Python onto the machine. In playbook syntax, the `become` option, to chose which user is going to run the task, does not work with the `raw` module, so we may need to add `sudo` in front of our commands when they require root permission.

A simple playbook to use this module might be as follows:

```
- name: run a simple command
  raw: echo "this was written by a raw Ansible
  module!!" >> ~/raw.txt
```

The command execution module

This module has the same function as the raw command module, but it is more optimized. It allows for multiple options and it has the capacity to use its return values for other tasks. As an example of a playbook, we will run a command and then collect its output for later use:

```
- name: run a simple command
  command: cat ~/raw.txt
  register: rawtxt

- debug: var=rawtxt.stdout
```

The output of the playbook will look as follows:

```
>alibi@alibi-ml ~/vagrant-ansible-lab> ansible-playbook  playbooks/modules_playbook.yml -v
Using /etc/ansible/ansible.cfg as config file

PLAY [Linux Module running] ******************************************************

TASK [run a simple command] ******************************************************
changed: [server2] => {"changed": true, "cmd": ["cat", "~/raw.txt"], "delta": "0:00:00.004157", "e
nd": "2018-07-15 17:06:25.883214", "rc": 0, "start": "2018-07-15 17:06:25.879057", "stderr": "", "
stderr_lines": [], "stdout": "this was written by a raw Ansible module!!", "stdout_lines": ["this
was written by a raw Ansible module!!"]}
changed: [server0] => {"changed": true, "cmd": ["cat", "~/raw.txt"], "delta": "0:00:00.003778", "e
nd": "2018-07-15 17:06:25.898959", "rc": 0, "start": "2018-07-15 17:06:25.895181", "stderr": "", "
stderr_lines": [], "stdout": "this was written by a raw Ansible module!!", "stdout_lines": ["this
was written by a raw Ansible module!!"]}
changed: [server1] => {"changed": true, "cmd": ["cat", "~/raw.txt"], "delta": "0:00:00.004177", "e
nd": "2018-07-15 17:06:25.899544", "rc": 0, "start": "2018-07-15 17:06:25.895367", "stderr": "", "
stderr_lines": [], "stdout": "this was written by a raw Ansible module!!", "stdout_lines": ["this
was written by a raw Ansible module!!"]}

TASK [debug] *********************************************************************
ok: [server0] => {
    "rawtxt.stdout": "this was written by a raw Ansible module!!"
}
ok: [server1] => {
    "rawtxt.stdout": "this was written by a raw Ansible module!!"
}
ok: [server2] => {
    "rawtxt.stdout": "this was written by a raw Ansible module!!"
}

PLAY RECAP **********************************************************************
server0                    : ok=2    changed=1    unreachable=0    failed=0
server1                    : ok=2    changed=1    unreachable=0    failed=0
server2                    : ok=2    changed=1    unreachable=0    failed=0
```

This module lacks the capacity to understand special environment variables, such as $PATH, Linux pipelining, and the redirection special characters. If this is necessary for your particular use case, use the next module on the list, shell.

The shell command module

This module is one of the handiest command modules. It not only allows you to run a command, it also runs shell scripts and allows you to specify the location for the working directory and the bash with which you want to execute the command line. By default, this module runs all its remote commands on the /bin/sh shell. The following playbook provides a good example:

```
- name: run a simple shell script
  shell: ./shell_script.sh >> ~/shell.txt
  args:
      chdir: /usr/local/
      creates: ~/shell.txt
      executable: /bin/csh
```

Shell also has several return values that are very useful.

The script execution module

This is another module to run a shell script on remote nodes. At first, however, it transfers the script that is located on the Ansible master to the remote hosts before executing them. The module runs the script on the shell environment of the remote host, just as if it were run by a local user on the host.

This module provides support for running other types of script, such as Python, Perl, or Ruby. Take a look at the following example playbook, which shows how to use it:

```
- name: execute a script on a remote host
  script: ./shell_script.py –some-argumets "42"
  args:
      creates: ~/shell.txt
      executable: python
```

This module acts like the raw command module. It is also supported on Windows remote hosts as it is.

The expect script module

If you are familiar with expect scripting, this is a module that is similar, but even simpler and on an even bigger scale. It is a way of dealing with interactive commands, such as password changing and SSH questions. An example of a playbook for changing a user password is as follows:

```
- name: change user1 password
  expect:
    command: passwd user1
    responses:
      (?i)password: "Ju5tAn07herP@55w0rd":
```

This module requires `pexpect` and `python` to be installed on the remote host.

Linux package modules

In this section, we will show two types of package managers: for operating systems and for programming languages.

Apt package manager module

This module manages packages for the Debian family, including Debian, Ubuntu, LinuxMint, KaliLinux, and so on. It requires you to have `aptitude`, `python-apt`, and `python3-apt` installed on the remote host to work. It has multiple options and functionalities to personalize package installation, removal, upgrade, and index update. The following playbook only shows some of its features:

```
- name: install some packages on a Debian OS
  apt:
      name: "{{ pkg }}"
      state: latest
      update_cache: yes
  vars:
      pkg:
      - aha
      - htop
```

This module has some extra complementary modules to help with extra repositories and the keys used for trusted certificates. It also has some special return values.

DNF package manager module

This module controls the new package manager for the Red Hat family, including Red Hat, Fedora, CentOS, and Scientific Linux. It helps to install, upgrade, remove, and search for packages in the local index. The following playbook shows how it can be used:

```
- name: install a package using dnf
  dnf:
      name: htop
      state: latest
```

This module requires you to have `python`, `python-dnf`, and `dnf` itself installed on the machine to work properly.

Yum package manager module

Yum is the original Red Hat package manager that is still in use today. It also has its own module that manages it. Just like `dnf`, it helps with managing packages and group packages. The following playbook shows how to enable a repository and then install a tool from it, using this module:

```
- name: add epel repo using yum
  yum:
      name: https://dl.fedoraproject.org/pub/epel
      /epel-release-latest-7.noarch.rpm
      state: present
  - name: install ansible using yum
    yum:
      name: ansible
      state: present
```

Homebrew package manager

Homebrew is the most famous open source package manager for macOS X. This module is made to help manage Homebrew packages remotely. A simple playbook can be used to remove a package on macOS X:

```
- name: remove a package using homebrew
  homebrew:
      name: htop
      state: absent
      update_homebrew: yes
```

PyPI Python package manager module

This is our first language package manager and probably the most famous. It manages Python packages and libraries. It has a variety of options that accommodate various different requirements that are related to Python libraries. To run this module we need to make sure that PyPI is installed on the remote hosts. The following example playbook will show some of them:

```
- name: install a python library from the default
repo
  pip:
     name: numpy
     version: 0.3
- name: install a python library from a github
  pip:
     name: https://github.com/jakubroztocil/httpie
     /archive/master.tar.gz
```

Cpanm Perl package manager module

Just like the `pip` module, this module manages the Perl package manager, **Comprehensive Perl Archive Network (CPAN)**. It is used in the same way; you can either install a library or package from the default repository or from an archive file located on the web or locally. To run this module, we need to make sure that `cpanminus` is installed on the remote hosts. This is shown in the example playbook, as follows:

```
- name: install a Perl library on a Linux host
  cpanm:
     name: IO
```

Linux file modules

Linux file management modules have some shared features that can be found in more than one module. You can use one module to perform a task that is composed of three different actions. In this section, we will be only talking about the major modules with a brief look at those that can perform similar functions as well.

File and folder management modules

The file module is basically the tool to manage everything to do with files and folder organization in terms of creation, removal, symlinks creation, permissions, and ownership.

We have linked the file module to the **access control list** (**ACL**) module, which is a module that only works on permission and ownership of files and folders on the Linux environment, to show that some tasks can be combined. This is shown in the following playbook:

```
- name: create a file with some specific acl
  file:
      path: /usr/local/script.py
      state: touch
      owner: user1
      group: developers
      mode: 0755
- name: change acl of a file
  acl:
      path: /usr/local/script.py
      entity: user2
      permission: w
      state: present
```

Data distribution modules (copy, unarchive, and get_url)

The `copy` module is used to transfer files from the Ansible master to the remote hosts or locally from within the remote host. This is followed by `unarchive`, which is an archive extractor that then transfers the files to the selected hosts. The `get_url` module basically downloads a file from a web location as an HTTP, HTTPS, or FTP file. The following playbook shows how each module can be used to achieve a goal:

```
- name: copy file from within a remote host
  copy:
      src: /usr/local/script.py
      dest: /home/user1/script.py
      remote_src: yes
      owner: user1
      group: developers
      mode: 0755
- name: extract an archive into remote hosts
  unarchive:
      src: ~/archive.tar.gz
      dest: /usr/local/
      owner: user1
      group: developers
      mode: 0755

- name: download an ansible archive to remote hosts
```

```
get_url:
    url: https://github.com/ansible/ansible/archive
    /v2.6.1.tar.gz
    dest: /usr/local/ansible_v2.6.1.tar.gz
    mode: 0777
```

The `copy` module supports having a backup option, which is very useful when copying configuration files; if there is an error, a user can always revert to the original. However, unarchive requires `gtar` and `unzip` to be installed on the master machine. All of these modules have special return values that show information about the status of the tasks.

Data collection module (fetch)

This is the module that reverses the previous module function. This module helps gather files from the remote hosts and stores them in the Ansible master machine. It can be handy when collecting apps and service logs, user configurations, or system related files. As an example, we will try to collect some files from each host and organize them in the master Ansible host:

```
- name: Collect user files from remote hosts
  fetch:
      src: /home/user1/.profile
      dest: /home/alibi/user1-profile-{{
       inventory_hostname }}
      flat: yes
```

This module is also supported when managing remote Windows hosts. It has a checksum validation process that can be deactivated for faster transfer at your own risk.

File editing modules (lineinfile, replace, and blockinfile)

These are the only three modules that you need to perform the great configuration file management skills that are had by tools, such as `awk` or `sed`. The `lineinfile` module looks for a specific line in a file and replaces it with a predefined regular expression. The `replace` module replaces all instances of a specific pattern within a file, and `blockinfile` inserts, modifies, or deletes one or several lines of text located between two marker lines in a file. We have merged these three modules together because they have similar basic functionalities, but each one is specialized with regard to how it does things. The following playbook example will show each of these modules used to deliver a specific task:

```
- name: change a sudo user to no longer need
  password with config testing
```

```
    lineinfile:
        path: /etc/sudoers
        regexp: '^%sudo\s'
        line: '%sudo ALL=(ALL) NOPASSWD: ALL'
        state: present
        validate: '/usr/sbin/visudo -cf %s'

  - name: change all static ethernet config to use a
    higher mtu
    replace:
        path: /etc/network/interfaces
        regexp: '^mtu 1400$'
        line: 'mtu 9000'
        backup: yes
        validate: 'systemd reload networking'

  - name: change a static ethernet configuration
    replace:
        path: /etc/network/interfaces
        block: |
            iface eth1 inet dhcp
                    dns-nameserver 8.8.8.8
                    dns-nameserver 8.8.4.4
                    mtu 9000
        backup: yes
        validate: 'systemd reload networking'
```

Linux networking modules

In this section, we are going to discover some of the Linux system network management modules.

Network interfaces management module

This module is a way to manage the /etc/network/interfaces file in Linux hosts. Basically, it allows you to create, modify, and remove a network interface configuration. This configuration is specific to each identified network interface; it does not change non-specified ones. The following playbook shows you how to perform a change for a specific interface:

```
  - name: Change mtu to 1500 for eth1 interface
    Interfaces_file:
        dest: /etc/network/interfaces
        iface: eth1
```

```
option: mtu
value: 1500
backup: yes
state: present
```

If this task gets its return values registered, the user can easily identify all the information about the after-change configuration of the interface.

For more advanced network management, check out the `nmcli` module. It can manage various connection and device types: Ethernet, teams, bonds, and VLANs.

Firewall UFW management module

This is an Ansible management module for the Linux firewall UFW. It basically manages ports, protocols, and IPS firewall permissions. An example playbook to enable a port on a specific protocol can be written as follows:

```
- name: add port 5000 for iperf testing on all hosts
  ufw:
      rule: allow
      port: 5000
      proto: tcp
```

This module requires `ufw`, as the command-line tool, to be installed on the remote hosts.

HAProxy control module

This is a module that manages HAProxy servers, commanding them to enable, disable, drain, and set weights for backend servers using socket commands. An example of a command to disable some HAProxy servers is as follows:

```
- name: disable a haproxy backend host
  haproxy:
      state: disabled
      host: '{{ inventory_hostname }}'
      socket: /usr/loca/haproxy/haproxy.sock
      backend: www
      wait: yes
```

Wake-on-LAN trigger module

This is a module that turns on hosts that are currently turned off. This feature requires Ansible to have already collected facts about the hosts and to be storing information about their MAC addresses. The following is a playbook code to show how this module can be used:

```
- name: start powered off hosts
  wakeonlan:
  mac: "{{ hostvars[inventory_hostname].ansible_default_ipv4.macaddress }}"
  port: 8
  delegate_to: localhost
```

Linux storage modules

Ansible does offer some Linux-specific storage devices and volume management.

File system management module

This module is most handy when dealing with a virtualized infrastructure, but it can also be used with a bare metal setup. A disk must already exist in a remote host before that host can manage it. In a virtual environment, Ansible or other management tools allow you to automatically add disks to the host and then manage them using this module. The following is an example of a playbook for formatting a disk using this module:

```
- name: create a filesystem from a newly added disk
  filesystem:
     fstype: ext4
     dev: /dev/sdc1
```

Check out the `lvg` and `lvol` modules for LVM volume and group management. LVM can simplify disk management when using a virtualized environment, especially when dealing with systems that require the shrinking and expansion of disk space.

Device mounting module

This can be a complimentary module to the file system. It is also very useful for managing volume mounting on a specific host system. This module manages `/etc/fstab`:

```
- name: mount the recently added volume to the system
  mount:
```

```
        path: /media/disk1
        fstype: ext4
        boot: yes
        state: mounted
        src: /dev/sdc1
```

This module can also handle mounting network drives. This may require you to install extra tools such as NFS and SMB client.

Disk partitioning module

This a module that controls the parted tools that help with device partitioning, collect their information, or save them as return values. The following example playbook shows how to remove a partition:

```
    - name: remove a no longer needed partition
      mount:
          device: /dev/sdc
          number: 1
          state: absent
```

GlusterFS control module

This is an Ansible module used to manage GlusterFS volumes across a cluster of hosts. It enables the user to add, delete, start, stop, and tune volumes on demand. The following example playbook shows how to create a new volume:

```
    - name: create a new GlusterFS volume
      gluster_volume:
          status: present
          name: gluster1
          bricks: /bridkes/brik1/g1
          rebalance: yes
          cluster:
             - 192.168.10.10
             - 192.168.10.11
             - 192.168.10.12
          run_once: true
```

Ansible Windows modules

Moving on from the Linux modules, let's now explore the modules that are used by Ansible to administrate Windows desktops and servers. Make sure to have already followed the preparation steps to ensure that the Windows hosts are ready to be controlled by Ansible.

Windows System Modules

Let's start by introducing the modules that control the Windows system and allow their users to manage its different aspects.

Windows user and group management module

These two modules are used to manage the users and groups of Windows hosts' local machines. The following playbook example shows how to add each mode to Windows hosts:

```
---
- name: Windows Module running
  hosts: winservers
  gather_facts: false
  tasks:
    - name: create a new group dev
      win_group:
        name: developers
        description: Development department group
        state: present

    - name: create a new user in the dev group
      win_user:
        name: winuser1
        password: Ju5t@n0th3rP@55w0rd
        state: present
        groups:
            - developers
```

Windows register editing module

Ansible offers remote management to the Windows hosts registry using the `win_regedit` module. This allows you to create, edit, and remove registry keys and their values. The following playbook shows how to disable Windows auto-update via the registry:

```
- name: disable Windows auto-update
  win_regedit:
     path: HKLM:SOFTWARE\Policies\Microsoft\Windows
     \WindowsUpdate\AU
     name: NoAutoUpdate
     data: 1
     type: binary
```

Windows service management module

This module allows Ansible users to manage and query Windows hosts services. The following Ansible playbook shows how we can disable Windows update services (not recommended, but handy to know):

```
- name: disable Windows update service
  win_service:
     name: wuauserv
     state: stopped
     start_mode: disabled
```

This module has return values that give information about the service status.

Windows updates and feature management modules (win_updates, win_hotfix, and win_feature)

Ansible manages Windows updates, hotfixes, and features using three complementary modules: `win_updates`, `win_hotfix` and `win_feature`. These modules use system default services and tools by commanding them to apply a set of tasks configured on a playbook. The following example playbook has three examples on how to use each of the modules to install or enable Microsoft tools, fixes, or features:

```
- name: install updates for Windows related
applications and tools
  win_updates:
     category_names:
        - Applications
        - Tools
     state: installed
     reboot: no
  become: yes
  become_user: SYSTEM
- name: install a specific Windows Hotfix
  win_hotfix:
     hotfix_kb: KB4088786
```

```
      source: C:\hotfixes\windows10.0-kb4088786-
    x64_7e3897394a48d5a915b7fbf59ed451be4b07077c.msu
      state: present

  - name: enable Hyper-V and Write Filter features
    win_feature:
      name:
          - Hyper-V
          - Unified-Write-Filter
      state: present
```

Special return values get generated by the execution of these modules. These are key features to automate the maintenance of Windows hosts.

 These three modules need to be run with the credentials of a user who is part of a domain or local administrator group.

Windows Wake-on-LAN trigger module

Just like the Linux host's Wake-on-LAN module, this module will start to shut down Windows hosts using their MAC addresses. An example Playbook is as follows:

```
  - name: start powered off Windows hosts
    win_wakeonlan:
      mac: "{{
hostvars[inventory_hostname].ansible_default_ipv4.macaddress }}"
      port: 8
    delegate_to: remote_system
```

This module will send a Wake-on-LAN magic packet to the specific MAC addressed. Only the hosts who are configured to accept the packet will respond. A BIOS or OS configuration to enable Wake-on-LAN is required.

Windows firewall management module

This module interacts with the Windows hosts' local firewall to configure its rules. This is shown by the following playbook, which enables the VNC protocol:

```
  - name: enable the VNC port on the host local
    firewall
    win_firewall_rule:
      name: VNC
```

```
localport: 5900
protocol: udp
direction: in
action: allow
state: present
enabled: yes
```

This module also needs to be executed by a local or domain administrator.

Windows package modules

Windows hosts application management can get complicated, compared to Linux and all the package managers that unify application installation in a few simple commands. Ansible uses its modules to bypass those challenges.

Chocolatey control module

Chocolatey is a third-party package manager for Windows systems. It allows its users to install, remove, and update a huge number of Windows applications using standard commands. Ansible provides a module that makes sure that Chocolatey is installed on the system, then starts using it to install the selected tools from its packages gallery (`https://chocolatey.org/packages`). The following is a sample playbook that shows a few multiple usages of the `win_chocolatey` module:

```
- name: setup the latest version of firefox
  win_chocolatey:
    name: firefox
    state: latest

- name: update all chocolatey installed tools
  win_chocolatey:
    name: all
    state: latest

- name: remove 7zip
  win_chocolatey:
    name: 7zip
    state: absent
```

Windows package manager

This is an Ansible module that is used to install and remove packages that are MSI or EXE files. It allows you to use a different source for the package, either on the local machine, on a network shared drive, or on the web. The following example playbook shows you how to install Atom:

```
- name: install atom editor on Windows hosts
  win_package:
    path: C:\app\atom.msi
    arguments: /install /norestart
    state: present
```

This module replaces old, unstable modules such as `win_msi`.

Windows command modules

Just like Linux, when there is a need to type your own command and there is no module that can simplify the task, a command module can make it easier. Ansible offers the following modules that allow you to send specific commands to remote Windows hosts.

Windows command modules (win_shell and win_command)

These two Ansible modules are the best way to send any PowerShell or bash commands to a Windows hosts. The `win_shell` module is more used for running scripts and long or multiline commands, while the command is more for running regular commands that may require extra parameters. The following playbook shows an example code:

```
- name: run a PowerShell script on a working
  directory
  win_shell: C:\scripts\PSscript.ps1
    args:
      chdir: C:\Users\winuser1\Workspace
- name: execute a PowerShell command on remote
  Windows hosts
  win_command: (get-service wuauserv | select status
   | Format-Wide | Out-String).trim()
  register: output

- debug: var=output.stdout
```

Windows task scheduling module

Windows hosts can be time-managed by scheduling future tasks using this module. It is a way to create, edit, and delete Windows-scheduled tasks. The following is an example of task scheduling on a playbook:

```
- name: schedule running a PowerShell script a
 specific time
  win_scheduled_task:
    name: PowerShellscript
    description: Run a script at a specific time
    actions:
    - path: C:\Windows\System32\WindowsPowerShell
      \v1.0\powershell.exe
      arguments: -ExecutionPolicy Unrestricted
    -NonInteractive -File
    triggers:
    - type: logon
   state: present
   enabled: yes
```

Windows file modules

Managing Windows hosts' files and folders is as simple as on a Linux system when using Ansible. It offers a set of modules that take care of all management needs.

Windows file and folder management module

This is a module to create, update, and remove files and folders on remote Windows hosts. This sample playbook shows how to manage a file and folder on a Windows system:

```
- name: add a new file
  win_file:
    path: C:\scripts\PSscript2.ps1
    state: touch
- name: remove a folder
  win_file:
    path: C:\scripts\TestScripts
    state: absent
```

This module does not change file permissions. To do this, you need to use the win_share module.

Windows data sharing module

This is a complementary module to `win_file`. This module sets modifies and removes shared permissions on Windows files and folders. This is a playbook showing a sample configuration for a specific folder on remote Windows hosts:

```
- name: add a new file
win_share:
name: devscript
description: Developers scripts shared folder
path: C:\scripts
list: yes
full: developers
read: devops
deny: marketing
```

This module is only supported on Windows 8 and Windows 2012 onward.

Windows file editing module

This is the Windows version of the Ansible module, `lineinfile`. It basically does the same job of changing a specific line if a file is based on a regular expression, but it is specifically for Windows hosts. The following is an example playbook:

```
- name: remove a folder
  win_lineinfile:
      path: C:\scripts\PSscript.ps1
      regexp: '^service='
      line: 'service=wuauserv'
```

Windows data sending modules (win_copy, win_robocopy, and win_get_url)

These are the modules that are responsible for transferring files to Windows remote hosts. Each has its own way to get the files to their destination. The `win_copy` module will copy the file either from the local machine or the remote host to a specific location in the remote hosts. The `win_robocopy` module works like `rsync` to synchronize the contents of two folders within the remote host. It can be very handy as a backup solution. The `win_get_url` module gets a URL as input to download the files into the specified location.

The following playbook shows some example cases:

```
- name: copy a file from one location to other within
  the Windows hosts
  win_copy:
      src: C:\scripts\PSscript.ps1
      dest: C:\applications\PSscript.ps1
      remote_src: yes

- name: backup scripts folder
  win_copy:
      src: C:\scripts\
      dest: D:\backup\scripts
      recurse: yes

- name: backup scripts folder
  win_get_url:
      url: https://www.github.com/scripts
      /winscript2.ps1
      dest: C:\scripts\ winscript2.ps1
```

Ansible network modules

Network device management has never been easier than with Ansible. Having a playbook, a unified language for all modules makes the management of proprietary network devices very simple and does not require you to learn vendor-specific tools and coding languages. Network administration is now part of the automated configuration management strategy.

This is a list of network proprietary devices currently supported by Ansible: Arista, Avi Networks, Cisco, Citrix NetScaler, Cumulus, Dell EMC, F5, Huawei, Infoblox, Juniper, Nokia, Mellanox, Lenovo, Palo Alto Networks, and Pluribus. We will not be able to cover all the modules that control these—this would probably require a book of its own!

 Being agentless, Ansible uses SSH and HTTPS to communicate with devices.

For this section, we will only cover the Cisco standard devices. We need to create a special inventory for them:

```
[ciscosw]
switch0          ansible_hosts=192.168.10.250
switch1          ansible_hosts=192.168.10.251
```

```
switch2                ansible_hosts=192.168.10.252

[ciscosw:vars]
ansible_connection=network_cli
ansible_user=admin
ansible_become=yes
ansible_become_method=enable
ansible_network_os=ios
ansible_user=user1
ansible_ssh_pass= "ju5t@n0th3rp@55"
```

> There are other ways to hide clear text passwords from YAML files; we
> will take a look at them, in the coming chapters on Ansible Vault.

Network data transfer modules (net_get and network_put)

These two modules allow for an easier transfer of configuration files between the control host and multiple network devices. They can be handy for backup or centralized configuration. These modules rely on the functionality of the scp command to carry out the transfer. An example is shown in the following playbook:

```
---
- name: Network Module running
  hosts: ciscosw
  tasks:
    - name: backup a running configuration for a cisco
     switch
      net_get:
          src: running_cfg_{{ inventory_hostname }}.txt
```

Cisco IOS command module

This module helps its users to send commands to a Cisco device running IOS, either a router, a switch, an access-point, or firewall. This module also has the option of making the task wait for a condition before returning with a timeout. The following is an example of a playbook showing command execution on a Cisco device:

```
- name: check on the switch network interfaces status
  ios_command:
```

```
commands: show interfaces brief
wait_for: result[0] contains Loopback0
```

Cisco ISO system configuration module

This module allows its user to modify the IOS running configuration of a Cisco device. The following example playbook will show how we can alter some configurations of the Cisco switch:

```
- name: change switch hostname to match the one set in the inventory
  ios_config:
      ines: hostname {{ inventory_hostname }}

- name: change IP helper config for DHCP requests sent into the device
  ios_config:
      lines: ip helper-address 192.168.10.1
```

Cisco IOS interface management module

This module manages the interface configuration of the Cisco network switches. In the following simple playbook, we will configure an interface and enable it:

```
- name: configure a gigabit interface and make ready to use
  ios_interface:
      name: GigabitEthernet0/1
      description: lab-network-link
      duplex: full
      speed: 1000
      mtu: 9000
      enabled: True
      state: up
```

Cisco IOS static route control module

As its name states, this module manages static route configuration on a Cisco network device. We will set a static route switch in the following example playbook:

```
- name: setup a static route on CISCO switches
  ios_static_route:
      prefix: 192.168.11.0
      mask: 255.255.255.0
      next_hop: 192.168.10.1
      state: present
```

Cisco IOS VLAN management module

This module allows the configuration of VLANs on a Cisco switch. This sample playbook shows how to add some network interfaces to a VLAN:

```
- name: Add new lab VLAN
  ios_vlan:
      vlan_id: 45
      name: lab-vlan
      state: present

- name: Add network interface to the lab VLAN
  ios_vlan:
      vlan_id: 45
      nterfaces:
          - GigabitEthernet0/1
          - GigabitEthernet0/2
```

Ansible cloud modules

Ansible has made managing virtualized and on cloud infrastructures very easy. It has over 300 modules that run several APIs designed to cover a variety of cloud providers, such as Amazon Web Services, Google Cloud Platform, OpenStack, Microsoft Azure, Digital Ocean, and Linode. These modules manage multiple aspects of the environment, including the hosts' operating systems, network connectivity, compute resources, and hosts provisioning.

When using Ansible modules with a cloud or virtual environment, it is recommended that you use a dynamic inventory for better management.

VMware modules

Ansible offers a list of modules to enable VMware infrastructure automated management.

We need to have the pyVmomi Python SDK installed:

```
pip install pyvmomi
```

These modules are built to manage the VMware ESX, ESXi, and vCenter server. In this section, we will describe some of the most useful modules that are involved in managing the VMware infrastructure.

An inventory file is required to host some of the data centre information:

```
---
[vms:vars]
datacenter: "vcenter.lab.edu"
vcenter_hostname: "vcenter.lab.edu"
vcenter_username: "admin"
vcenter_password: "@dm1np@55w0rd"

[vms]
vm0
vm1
vm2

[esxi_hostname]
esxihost1          esxihost1.lab.edu
esxihost2          esxihost2.lab.edu
```

VMware guest management modules (vmware_guest and vsphere_guest)

This module allows the creation, modification, and removal of virtual machines. They also allow status and resource control of the specified virtual machines, including power status modification and they complement customization. The following playbook example shows how to create a virtual machine based on a template:

```
---
- name: VMware Module running
  hosts: vms
  tasks:
    - name: create a new virtual machine from a template
      vmware_guest:
          hostname: "{{ vcenter_hostname }}"
          username: "{{ vcenter_username }}"
          password: "{{ vcenter_password }}"
          validate_certs: False
          folder: /lab-folder
        name: "{{ inventory_hostname }}"
        state: poweredon
        template: debian8_temp
        disk:
        - size_gb: 15
          type: thin
          datastore: labdatastore1
        hardware:
          memory_mb: 1024
```

```
num_cpus: 2
num_cpu_cores_per_socket: 2
scsi: paravirtual
max_connections: 5
hotadd_cpu: True
hotremove_cpu: True
hotadd_memory: True
hotremove_memory: True
version: 11
cdrom:
    type: iso
    iso_path: "[ labdatastore1] /iso_folder/debian8.iso"
networks:
- name: Lab Network
wait_for_ip_address: yes
delegate_to: localhost
```

The `vsphere_guest` module does the same job as `vmware_guest`, but it is a legacy module that is less stable and does not support as many features as `vmare_guest`.

VMware guest snapshot management module

This Ansible module enables automatic snapshot management of virtual machines. The following playbook example shows how to take a snapshot on virtual machines:

```
- name: create a virtual machine snapshot
  vmware_guest_snapshot:
      hostname: "{{ vcenter_hostname }}"
      username: "{{ vcenter_username }}"
      password: "{{ vcenter_password }}"
      datacentre: vcenter.lab.edu
      validate_certs: False
      folder: /lab-folder
      name: "{{ inventory_hostname }}"
      state: present
      snapshot_name: Post_Fixes
      description: Fixes_done_on_vm
  delegate_to: localhost
```

Case sensitivity is very important when dealing with VMware modules, especially when dealing with virtual machine snapshots. When calling the snapshot later, ensure that its name is exactly the same.

VMware virtual machine shell execution module

The following module allows its user to run commands on the virtual machine's operating system via the use of the VMware tools:

```
- name: run a command on a running virtual machine
  vmware_guest_snapshot:
      hostname: "{{ vcenter_hostname }}"
      username: "{{ vcenter_username }}"
      password: "{{ vcenter_password }}"
      datacentre: vcenter.lab.edu
      validate_certs: False
      folder: /lab-folder
      vm_id: "{{ inventory_hostname }}"
      vm_username: setup
      vm_password: "@P@55w0rd"
      vm_shell: /bin/service
      vm_shell_args: networking restart
  delegate_to: localhost
```

VMware host power state control module

This module manages the physical equipment of the VMware infrastructure. The ESX/ESXi hosts are where the computer resources are stored. This module manages the power status of the hosts. It can very handy when scheduling a reboot after maintenance, an update, or a fix. The following example playbook shows how this module can be used:

```
- name: restart ESXi host
  vmware_guest_snapshot:
      hostname: "{{ vcenter_hostname }}"
      username: "{{ vcenter_username }}"
      password: "{{ vcenter_password }}"
      validate_certs: no
      esxi_hostname: esxihost1.lab.edu
      state: reboot-host
  delegate_to: localhost
```

Docker modules

The recent versions of Ansible have introduced several modules dedicated to Docker container management. To be able to use the Docker's Ansible modules, the management hosts should have the following Python packages installed:

```
pip install 'docker-py>=1.7.0'

pip install 'docker-compose>=1.7.0'
```

It is best to use a dynamic inventory when working with Docker containers.

 Ansible has recently introduced a new feature to enable building containers without the use of Dockerfiles. The `ansible-container` module builds containers and orchestrates the deployment via playbooks.

Docker container management module

This module manages the life cycle of a Docker container running on either on a local machine or other hosts. The following playbook shows how this module works:

```
---
- name: Docker Module running
  hosts: local
  tasks:
    - name: create a container
      docker_container:
          name: debianlinux
          image: debian:9
          pull: yes
          state: present

    - name: start a container
      docker_container:
          name: debianlinux
          state: started
          devices:
             - "/dev/sda:/dev/xvda:rwm"
    - name: stop a container
      docker_container:
          name: debianlinux
          state: stopped
```

Docker image management module

This module is useful for container developers. It helps with building, loading, pulling, and pushing container images to a repository or archiving a container into a tar file. The following playbook example shows some possible tasks that can be carried out with this module:

```
- name: pull a container image
  docker_image:
      name: ubuntu:18.04
      pull: yes

- name: push a container image to docker hub
  docker_image:
      name: labimages/ubuntu
      repository: labimages/ubuntu
      tag: lab18
      push: yes

- name: remove a container image
  docker_image:
      name: labimages/ubuntu
      state: absent
      tag: lab16
```

Docker login module

This module allows the user to log in to DockerHub or a private repository. The following playbook shows how this can be done:

```
- name: login to DockerHub
  docker_login:
      username: labuser1
      password: "L@bp@55w0rd"
      email: user1@lab.edu
```

Amazon AWS modules

Ansible allows automation of your AWS cloud environment, enabling dynamic provisioning of instances and smart scalability via the huge number of modules dedicated to AWS services. In this section, we will only focus on Amazon AWS EC2. There is a large library of modules to manage other AWS services and services for other cloud providers that can be found on the Ansible module index.

As a prerequisite, it is highly recommended that you have a dynamic inventory. It is also recommended that you store the access and secret keys in `vars_file` and possibly protect them using Ansible Vault:

```
---
ec2_access_key: "a_key"
ec2_secret_key: "another_key"
```

You are also required to install the `boto` Python library on the controlling machine to interact with AWS Services:

```
pip install boto
```

AWS EC2 instance management module

This module allows the creation and termination of AWS EC2 instances. The following playbook shows how to create a new AWS EC2 instance:

```
---
- name: AWS Module running
  hosts: localhost
  gather_facts: False
  tasks:
    - name: create a new AWS EC2 instance
      ec2:
          key_name: ansible_key
          instance_type: t2.micro
          image: ami-6b3fd60c
          wait: yes
          group: labservers
          count: 2
          vpc_subnet_id: subnet-3ba41052
          assign_public_ip: yes
```

AWS WC2 AMI management module

This module helps register new EC2 AMI images to be used for instance creation later. It also allows you to deregister old images when they are no longer needed. The following example playbook shows how to register an EC2 AMI image:

```
    - name: register an AWS AMI image
      ec2_ami:
          instance_id: i-6b3fd61c
          wait: yes
          name: labami
```

```
tags:
    Name: LabortoryImage
    Service: LabScripts
```

AWS EC2 key management module

This module helps with the management of an EC2 key pair. It helps to create and remove keys. The following example playbook shows you how to create a key:

```
- name: create an EC@ key pair
  ec2_key:
      name: ansible2-key
      key_material: "{{ lookup('file', '/home/admin
      /.ssh/id_rsa') }}"
      state: present
```

Summary

In this chapter, we have tried to show you as many useful modules as possible, with examples of daily activities that can be carried out and personal comments based on our experience of using them. Further modules and more advanced features can be found in the official Ansible documentation. Here, we have only discussed modules that are officially supported and maintained; it would be impossible to cover all of the modules that are available in the community, on the Ansible Galaxy platform, or in the entire range of GitHub projects. If you can think of a task that I have not discussed in this chapter, rest assured that somebody out there will have a bug or a fix to make it happen. Ansible has one of the biggest communities in the open source world; feel free to use it.

In the next chapter, we are going to use some of these tools to carry out some real automation. We will be mixing and matching various modules in playbooks to perform a complex playbook for the usual daily tasks.

References

- Ansible official documentation website: `https://docs.ansible.com/`
- Ansible Module Index: `https://docs.ansible.com/ansible/latest/modules/list_of_all_modules.html`
- Chocolatey Packages Gallery: `https://chocolatey.org/packages`

5
Ansible Automated Infrastructure

We have covered how to code playbooks and how to properly populate them with some handy modules. Now let's mix everything together and build real-life daily infrastructure management situations. This chapter will provide a series of examples in which we are going to use Ansible playbooks, with the help of some Linux tools. This will help automate daily tasks and other tasks that happen out of hours. These playbooks will have multiple tasks that work in sequence to allow you to plan your work efficiently.

This chapter will cover the following topics:

- Automation of Linux systems and applications
- Automation of Windows systems and applications
- Management of container configuration
- Automation of network configuration
- Automation of virtual and cloud infrastructure

Linux infrastructure automation

We are going to start by looking at various use cases that involve Linux administration. In this section, we are going to identify a task that is usually done manually and try to automate as much of it as possible. An administrator may still be required in situations where there are errors or misconfiguration.

We are going to divide the following use cases into subcategories to better identify their role in general. In each case, we will look at several Ansible tasks. These will either follow a playbook sequence, be executed if certain conditions are met, or be carried out within a loop.

System management automation

Within this subsection, we are going to show some use cases involving system administration tasks that can be automated using Ansible playbooks. We will first describe the task and the environment in which it will be executed and then we will write a well-formatted and named playbook to illustrate how Ansible can be used.

Use case 1 – system update automation

This use case is built to update and clean a Linux-based host under the two main families: Debian and Red Hat. The task should be able to update the software list index, install any available updates, remove unnecessary packages, clean the package manager cache, and, finally, restart the hosts if required. This playbook can be used on either physical or virtual Linux hosts that are accessible to the Ansible management server.

The code for this playbook is as follows:

```
---
- name: Update and clean up Linux OS
  hosts: Linux
  become: yes
  gather_facts: yes
  tasks:
    - name: Update Debian Linux packages with Index
      updated
      apt:
        upgrade: dist
        update_cache: yes
      when: ansible_os_family == "Debian"

    - name: Update Red Hat Linux packages with Index
      updated
      yum:
        name: "*"
        state: latest
        update_cache: yes
      when: ansible_os_family == "RedHat"

    - name: Clean up Debian Linux from cache and unused
      packages
      apt:
        autoremove: yes
        autoclean: yes
      when: ansible_os_family == "Debian"
```

```
    - name: Clean up Red Hat Linux from cache and unused
      packages
      shell: yum clean all; yum autoremove
      when: ansible_os_family == "RedHat"
      ignore_errors: yes

  - name: Check if Debian system requires a reboot
    shell: "[ -f /var/run/reboot-required ]"
    failed_when: False
    register: reboot_required
    changed_when: reboot_required.rc == 0
    notify: reboot
    when: ansible_os_family == "Debian"
    ignore_errors: yes

  - name: Check if Red Hat system requires a reboot
    shell: "[ $(rpm -q kernel|tail -n 1) !=
    kernel-$(uname -r) ]"
    failed_when: False
    register: reboot_required
    changed_when: reboot_required.rc == 0
    notify: reboot
    when: ansible_os_family == "RedHat"
    ignore_errors: yes

handlers:
  - name: reboot
    command: shutdown -r 1 "A system reboot triggered
    after and Ansible automated system update"
    async: 0
    poll: 0
    ignore_errors: true
```

This playbook can then be scheduled to be executed using the `crontab` job during weekends or late at night when the system is idle. Alternatively, it can be scheduled to run during a maintenance period for a system that is active all the time. To accommodate redundant hosts, the user can add a batch size and a maximum failure percentage parameter to the playbook header, before defining the tasks. The following lines of code can be used to enable a level of protection:

```
---
- name: Update and clean up Linux OS
  hosts: Linux
  max_fail_percentage: 20
  serial: 5
  become: yes
  become_user: setup
```

```
gather_facts: yes
tasks: ...
```

This allows you to work on five hosts at a time. In the event of 20% failure on the total amount of hosts, the playbook stops.

Use case 2 – creating a new user with all its settings

This use case allows you to automate the addition of a new user to your system. Basically, we are going to create a new user in all Linux hosts, with the password already set up. We are also going to create an SSH key so that it can be accessed remotely and add some sudo configurations for easier management. This is implemented in the following code:

```
---
- name: Create a dedicated remote management user
  hosts: Linux
  become: yes
  gather_facts: yes
  tasks:
    - name: Create a now basic user
      user:
        name: 'ansuser'
        password:
$6$C2rcmXJPhMAxLLEM$N.XOWkuukX7Rms7QlvclhWIOz6.MoQd/
jekgWRgDaDH5oU2OexNtRYPTWwQ2lcFRYYevM83wIqrK76sgnVqOX.
        # A hash for generic password.
        append: yes
        groups: sudo
        shell: /bin/bash
        state: present

    - name: Create the user folder to host the SSH key
      file:
        path: /home/ansuser/.ssh
        state: directory
        mode: 0700
        owner: ansuser

    - name: Copy server public SSH key to the newly
      created folder
      copy:
        src: /home/admin/.ssh/ansible_rsa
        dest: /home/ansuser/.ssh/id_rsa
        mode: 0600
        owner: ansuser
```

```
- name: Configure the sudo group to work without a
  password
  lineinfile:
      dest: /etc/sudoers
      regexp: '^%sudo\s'
      line: "%sudo ALL=(ALL) NOPASSWD{{':'}} ALL"
      validate: 'visudo -cf %s'
      state: present

- name: Install favourite text editor for Debian
  family
  apt:
      name: nano
      state: latest
      update_cache: yes
  when: ansible_os_family == "Debian"

- name: Install favourite text editor for Red Hat
  family
  yum:
      name: nano
      state: latest
  when: ansible_os_family == "RedHat"

- name: remove old editor configuration file
  file:
      path: /home/ansuser/.selected_editor
      state: absent
  ignore_errors: yes

- name: Create a new configuration file with the
  favorite text editor
  lineinfile:
      dest: /home/ansuser/.selected_editor
      line: "SELECTED_EDITOR='/usr/bin/nano'"
      state: present
      create: yes

- name: Make the user a system user to hide it from
  login interface
  blockinfile:
      path: /var/lib/AccountsService/users/ansuser
      state: present
      create: yes
      block: |
          [User]
          SystemAccount=true
```

When executed on the right inventory configuration, this playbook should be able to replace the hours' worth of work that is usually involved in accessing multiple hosts to configure a single user. It is possible to add additional capabilities to any playbook with some tweaking. In this case, we can add any user configuration to a pipeline.

Use case 3 – services (systemd) management

In this use case, we will use an Ansible playbook to automatically set up and configure some system services on multiple hosts. The following lines of code show how to make sure a service is installed and then how to carry out a configuration check to make sure it is well-configured. Finally, we start the service and enable it to start upon system startup:

```
---
- name: Setup and configured recommended Linux services
  hosts: Linux
  become: yes
  gather_facts: yes
  tasks:
    - name: Install a list of services on Linux hosts
      package:
          name: '{{ item }}'
          state: latest
      with_items:
          - ntp
          - tzdate
          - autofs

    - name: Fix time zone on Red Hat 6
      lineinfile:
          path: /etc/sysconfig/clock
          line: "ZONE='Europe/London'"
          state: present
          create: yes
      when: ansible_os_family == 'RedHat' and
      ansible_distribution_version.split('.')[0] == '6'

    - name: Setup time zone on all local hosts
      timezone:
          name: "Europe/London"

    - name: Fix time zone on Red Hat 6
      blockinfile:
          path: /etc/ntp.conf
          block: |
              server time.nist.gov iburst
              server 0.uk.pool.ntp.org iburst
```

```
          server 1.uk.pool.ntp.org iburst
        insertafter: "# Specify one or more NTP
        servers."
        state: present
    when: ansible_os_family == 'RedHat'

- name: Restart NTP service to apply change and enable
  it on Debian
  systemd:
  name: ntp
  enabled: True
  state: restarted
  when: ansible_os_family == 'Debian'

- name: Restart NTP service to apply change and enable
  it on Red Hat
  systemd:
  name: ntpd
  enabled: True
  state: restarted
  when: ansible_os_family == 'RedHat'

- name: Add NFS and SMB support to automount
  blockinfile:
  path: /etc/auto.master
  block: |
  /nfs /etc/auto.nfs
  /cifs /etc/auto.cifs
  state: present

- name: create the NFS and SMB AutoFS configuration
  files
  file:
  name: '{{ item }}'
  state: touch
  with_items:
  - '/etc/auto.nfs'
  - '/etc/auto.cifs'

- name: Restart AutoFS service to apply a change and
  enable it
  systemd:
  name: autofs
  enabled: True
  state: restarted
```

This playbook can be called by another playbook as part of a provisioning task to configure the hosts after they are built. It is also possible to add extra functionalities to enable aspects of a bigger Ansible role.

Use case 4 – automated network drive mounting (NFS, SMB)

We are now going to set up some remote hosts to be NFS and SMB clients. We will also configure some drives to connect to automatically using AutoFS, which was installed in an earlier use case. The following lines of code install the dependencies, configure the clients, and then start the services. This playbook works with both Debian and Red Hat Linux families:

```
---
- name: Setup and connect network shared folders
  hosts: Linux
  become: yes
  gather_facts: yes
  tasks:
    - name: Install the dependencies to enable NFS and
      SMB clients on Linux Debian family
      apt:
        name: '{{ item }}'
        state: latest
      with_items:
        - nfs-common
        - rpcbind
        - cifs-utils
        - autofs
      when: ansible_os_family == 'Debian'

    - name: Install the dependencies to enable NFS and
      SMB clients on Linux Red Hat family
      yum:
        name: '{{ item }}'
        state: latest
      with_items:
        - nfs-common
        - rpcbind
        - cifs-utils
        - nfs-utils
        - nfs-utils-lib
        - autofs
      when: ansible_os_family == 'RedHat'
```

```
- name: Block none authorised NFS servers using
  rpcbind
  lineinfile:
      path: /etc/hosts.deny
      line: "rpcbind: ALL"
      state: present
      create: yes

- name: Allow the target NFS servers using rpcbind
  lineinfile:
      path: /etc/hosts.allow
      line: "rpcbind: 192.168.10.20"
      state: present
      create: yes

- name: Configure NFS share on Fstab
  mount:
      name: nfs shared
      path: /nfs/shared
      src: "192.168.10.20:/media/shared"
      fstype: nfs
      opts: defaults
      state: present

- name: Create the shared drive directories
  file:
      name: '{{ item }}'
      state: directory
      with_items:
      - '/nfs/shared'
      - '/cifs/winshared'

- name: Configure NFS share on AutoFS
  lineinfile:
      path: /etc/auto.nfs
      line: "shared -fstype=nfs,rw,
      192.168.10.20:/media/shared"
      state: present

- name: Configure SMB share on AutoFS
  lineinfile:
      path: /etc/auto.cifs
      line: "winshared
      -fstype=cifs,rw,noperm,credentials=/etc/crd.txt
       ://192.168.11.20/winshared"
      state: present

- name: Restart AutoFS service to apply NFS and SMB
```

```
                        changes
                        systemd:
                            name: autofs
                            state: restarted
```

This playbook can be personalized, as is the case for any playbook. For example, it can be scheduled to run after the playbook that is responsible for setting up the shared drive servers.

Use case 5 – automated backup of important documents

In this use case, we are trying to build a backup solution that does not use too much of the bandwidth by archiving everything that needs to be backed up. We are basically going to select a folder to be compressed and moved to a secure host. The following code makes sure that all the necessary dependencies are installed, prepares the backup folder, compresses it, and then sends it. We are going to use a module called synchronize, which is basically a wrapper around `rsync`, the famous data synchronization tool. It is frequently used to provide a quick backup solution:

```
---
- name: Setup and connect network shared folders
  hosts: Linux
  become: yes
  gather_facts: yes
  tasks:
    - name: Install the dependencies to for archiving the
      backup
      package:
          name: '{{ item }}'
          state: latest
      with_items:
          - zip
          - unzip
          - gunzip
          - gzip
          - bzip2
          - rsync

    - name: Backup the client folder to the vault
      datastore server
      synchronize:
          mode: push
          src: /home/client1
          dest: client@vault.lab.edu:/media/vault1/client1
```

```
            archive: yes
            copy_links: yes
            delete: no
            compress: yes
            recursive: yes
            checksum: yes
            links: yes
            owner: yes
            perms: yes
            times: yes
            set_remote_user: yes
            private_key: /home/admin/users_SSH_Keys/id_rsa
        delegate_to: "{{ inventory_hostname }}"
```

This playbook can be added to a `crontab` job to schedule regular backups to a specific folder.

Automation of applications and service

This subsection is not too dissimilar from the previous one, but it focuses on the applications and services that are provided by the system to the outside world, rather than on those that are related to the host's internal system management. Here, we will present some use cases that handle tasks related to applications or services automatically.

Use case 1 – setting up a Linux desktop environment with some pre-installed tools

Linux administration is not limited to administrating servers. Nowadays, Linux GUI users are on the rise, due to the emergence of new scientific research and other sophisticated tools that are being developed to work better in a Linux environment. Some of these tools do require the Terminal to be used, but there are others that require a GUI interface, for example, to show a 3D-rendered molecular structure. In this first use case, we are going to make a playbook that ensures that Linux hosts have all the required tools for specific uses. This script will install a simple Linux graphical interface, Openbox. This script is only compatible with Linux systems from the Debian family, but it can be easily converted to support the Red Hat family, too.

The following playbook code includes multiple ways of setting up applications in a Linux environment:

```
    ---
    - name: Setup and connect network shared folders
```

```
hosts: Linux
become: yes
gather_facts: yes
tasks:
  - name: Install OpenBox graphical interface
    apt:
      name: '{{ item }}'
      state: latest
      update_cache: yes
    with_items:
      - openbox
      - nitrogen
      - pnmixer
      - conky
      - obconf
      - xcompmgr
      - tint2

  - name: Install basic tools for desktop Linux usage
    and application build
    apt:
      name: '{{ item }}'
      state: latest
      update_cache: yes
    with_items:
      - htop
      - screen
      - libreoffice-base
      - libreoffice-calc
      - libreoffice-impress
      - libreoffice-writer
      - gnome-tweak-tool
      - firefox
      - thunderbird
      - nautilus
      - build-essential
      - automake
      - autoconf
      - unzip
      - python-pip
      - default-jre
      - cmake
      - git
      - wget
      - cpanminus
      - r-base
      - r-base-core
      - python3-dev
```

```
        - python3-pip
        - libgsl0-dev

  - name: Install tools using Perl CPAN
    cpanm:
        name: '{{ item }}'
    with_items:
        - Data::Dumper
        - File::Path
        - Cwd

  - name: Install tools using Python PyPip
    shell: pip3 install -U '{{ item }}'
    with_items:
        - numpy
        - cython
        - scipy
        - biopython
        - pandas

  - name: Install tools on R CRAN using Bioconductor as
    source
    shell: Rscript --vanilla -e
      "source('https://bioconductor.org/biocLite.R');
      biocLite(c('ggplots2', 'edgeR','optparse'),
      ask=FALSE);"

  - name: Download a tool to be compiled on each host
    get_url:
        url: http://cegg.unige.ch/pub/newick-utils-1.6-
        Linux-x86_64-enabled-extra.tar.gz
        dest: /usr/local/newick.tar.gz
        mode: 0755

  - name: Unarchive the downloaded tool on each host
    unarchive:
        src: /usr/local/newick.tar.gz
        dest: /usr/local/
        remote_src: yes
        mode: 0755

  - name: Configure the tool before to the host before
    building
    command: ./configure chdir="/usr/local/newick-
    utils-1.6"

  - name: Build the tool on the hosts
    make:
```

```
        chdir: /usr/local/newick-utils-1.6
        target: install

  - name: Create Symlink to the tool's binary to be
    executable from anywhere in the system
    shell: ln -s -f /usr/local/newick-utils-1.6/src
        /nw_display /usr/local/bin/nw_display

  - name: Installing another tool located into a github
    repo
    git:
        repo: https://github.com/chrisquince/DESMAN.git
        dest: /usr/local/DESMAN
        clone: yes

  - name: Setup the application using python compiler
    command: cd /usr/local/DESMAN; python3 setup.py install
```

This playbook can be executed after several hosts are deployed, either by calling it after the first script has finished or by setting up a watch script to wait for a specific host to be available to start this playbook.

Use case 2 – LAMP server setup and configuration

This use case automates a task that is usually carried out by system administrators manually. Using the following playbook, we are going to set up a LAMP server, which is basically a web server, Apache2; a content manager PHP; and a database manager, MySQL server. We will also add some plugins and configuration that adhere to best practice standards. The following script only works with the Debian Linux family:

```
---
- name: Install a LAMP on Linux hosts
  hosts: webservers
  become: yes
  gather_facts: yes
  tasks:
    - name: Install Lamp packages
      apt:
          name: '{{ item }}'
          state: latest
          update_cache: yes
      with_items:
          - apache2
          - mysql-server
          - php
          - libapache2-mod-php
```

```
            - python-mysqldb

- name: Create the Apache2 web folder
  file:
      dest: "/var/www"
      state: directory
      mode: 0700
      owner: "www-data"
      group: "www-data"

- name: Setup Apache2 modules
  command: a2enmod {{ item }} creates=/etc/apache2
  /mods-enabled/{{ item }}.load
  with_items:
      - deflate
      - expires
      - headers
      - macro
      - rewrite
      - ssl

- name: Setup PHP modules
  apt:
      name: '{{ item }}'
      state: latest
      update_cache: yes
  with_items:
      - php-ssh2
      - php-apcu
      - php-pear
      - php-curl
      - php-gd
      - php-imagick
      - php-mcrypt
      - php-mysql
      - php-json

- name: Remove MySQL test database
  mysql_db:   db=test state=absent login_user=root
  login_password="DBp@55w0rd"

- name: Restart mysql server
  service:
      name: mysql
      state: restarted

- name: Restart Apache2
  service:
```

```
      name: apache2
      state: restarted
```

This playbook can be personalized by modifying some of the configuration files and populating the Apache2 web folder.

Windows infrastructure automation

Using Ansible playbooks, it is just as easy to automate a Windows infrastructure as it is to automate a Linux one. In this section, we are going to explore some use cases in which we are going to automate some Windows administration tasks.

 These use cases are tested on Windows 10. Extra configurations may be required to make them run on Windows 7 or 8.

System management automation

In this subsection, we are going to focus on use cases related to the management of the Windows system.

Use case 1 – system update automation

This use case tackles the automation of Windows host systems and some application updates. We are going to make updates restricted to what the playbook asks the hosts to do by disabling auto update and only updating the permitted categories:

```
---
- name: Windows updates management
  hosts: windows
  gather_facts: yes
  tasks:
    - name: Create the registry path for Windows Updates
      win_regedit:
        path: HKLM:\SOFTWARE\Policies\Microsoft\Windows
        \WindowsUpdate\AU
        state: present
      ignore_errors: yes

    - name: Add register key to disable Windows AutoUpdate
```

```
  win_regedit:
    path: HKLM:\SOFTWARE\Policies\Microsoft\Windows
   \WindowsUpdate\AU
    name: NoAutoUpdate
    data: 1
    type: dword
 ignore_errors: yes

- name: Make sure that the Windows update service is
  running
  win_service:
    name: wuauserv
    start_mode: auto
    state: started
  ignore_errors: yes

- name: Executing Windows Updates on selected
  categories
  win_updates:
    category_names:
      - Connectors
      - SecurityUpdates
      - CriticalUpdates
      - UpdateRollups
      - DefinitionUpdates
      - FeaturePacks
      - Application
      - ServicePacks
      - Tools
      - Updates
      - Guidance
    state: installed
    reboot: yes
  become: yes
  become_method: runas
  become_user: SYSTEM
  ignore_errors: yes
  register: update_result

- name: Restart Windows hosts in case of update
  failure
  win_reboot:
  when: update_result.failed
```

This playbook can be scheduled to be executed out of hours or during a scheduled maintenance period. The reboot module is used to handle Windows updates that fail the update module because they require a system restart. Usually, most updates will trigger the return value of `require_reboot` that initiates the restart of the machine after an update been installed.

Use case 2 – automated Windows optimization

This module is kind of a cleanup and organization of the system. It is primarily aimed at desktop Windows hosts, but some tasks can be used for servers.

This playbook will start by showing how to remote startup a Windows host that has been shut down. We then wait until it has properly powered on to do a disk defragmentation. After that, we perform some registry optimization tasks and finish by joining the host to a domain:

```
---
- name: Windows system configuration and optimisation
  hosts: windows
  gather_facts: yes
  vars:
    macaddress: "{{
    (ansible_interfaces|first).macaddress|default
    (mac|default('')) }}"
     tasks:
   - name: Send magic Wake-On-Lan packet to turn on
     individual systems
     win_wakeonlan:
       mac: '{{ macaddress }}'
       broadcast: 192.168.11.255

   - name: Wait for the host to start it WinRM service
     wait_for_connection:
       timeout: 20

   - name: start a defragmentation of the C drive
     win_defrag:
       include_volumes: C
       freespace_consolidation: yes

   - name: Setup some registry optimization
     win_regedit:
       path: '{{ item.path }}'
       name: '{{ item.name }}'
       data: '{{ item.data|default(None) }}'
```

```
    type: '{{ item.type|default("dword") }}'
    state: '{{ item.state|default("present") }}'
  with_items:
# Set primary keyboard layout to English (UK)
- path: HKU:\.DEFAULT\Keyboard Layout\Preload
  name: '1'
  data: 00000809
  type: string

# Show files extensions on Explorer
- path: HKCU:\Software\Microsoft\Windows
  \CurrentVersion\Explorer\Advanced
  name: HideFileExt
  data: 0

# Make files and folders search faster on the
  explorer
- path: HKCU:\Software\Microsoft\Windows
 \CurrentVersion\Explorer\Advanced
  name: Start_SearchFiles
  data: 1

- name: Add Windows hosts to local domain
  win_domain_membership:
    hostname: '{{ inventory_hostname_short }}'
    dns_domain_name: lab.edu
    domain_ou_path: lab.edu
    domain_admin_user: 'admin'
    domain_admin_password: '@dm1nP@55'
    state: domain
```

Application and services automation

In this subsection, we will focus on use cases related to Windows applications that are available on the Chocolatey repository and others that we would like to install traditionally for a variety of reasons.

Use case 1 – automating Windows application management

Application management on a Windows machine can be a bit messy since Windows has always lacked a package manager. Chocolatey is one of the solutions that can help fix this issue. The following playbook code makes sure that all the requirements for Chocolatey are installed, then checks for updates to all the application that are installed by Chocolatey. Finally, it installs the latest version of new applications.

 It is advised to use this use case with desktop-based Windows hosts rather than for servers. It can be used on servers, however, since most Windows servers now have a graphical interface too.

The following playbook code shows how the preceding actions can be carried out:

```
---
- name: Application management on Windows hosts
  hosts: windows
  gather_facts: yes
  tasks:
   - name: Install latest updated PowerShell for
    optimized Chocolatey commands
     win_chocolatey:
        name: powershell
        state: latest

   - name: Update Chocolatey to its latest version
     win_chocolatey:
        name: chocolatey
        state: latest

   - name: Install a list of applications via Chocolatey
     win_chocolatey:
        name: "{{ item }}"
        state: latest
     with_items:
        - javaruntime
        - flashplayeractivex
        - 7zip
        - firefox
        - googlechrome
        - atom
        - notepadplusplus
        - vlc
        - adblockplus-firefox
```

```
      - adblockplus-chrome
      - adobereader
  ignore_errors: yes
```

 A more extensive list of applications is available on the Chocolatey packages index web page (`https://chocolatey.org/packages`).

This playbook can be used to set up a generic image for specific users who use a number of specific applications on a regular basis.

Use case 2 – setting up an NSclient Nagios client

We always introduce new equipment to a certain environment. One of the tasks that is required to set up a new host properly is to link it to the monitoring system. For this use case, we are going to show how to set up a Nagios agent in a Windows host and configure it from a sample configuration file:

```
---
- name: Setup Nagios agent on Windows hosts
  hosts: windows
  gather_facts: yes
  tasks:
    - name: Copy the MSI file for the NSClient to the
      windows host
      win_copy:
        src: ~/win_apps/NSCP-0.5.0.62-x64.msi
        dest: C:\NSCP-0.5.0.62-x64.msi

    - name: Install an NSClient with the appropriate
      arguments
      win_msi:
        path: C:\NSCP-0.5.0.62-x64.msi
        extra_args:
ADDLOCAL=FirewallConfig,LuaScript,DotNetPluginSupport,Documentation,CheckPl
ugins,NRPEPlugins,NSCPlugins,NSCAPlugin,PythonScript,ExtraClientPlugin,Samp
leScripts ALLOWED_HOSTS=127.0.0.1,192.168.10.10 CONF_NSCLIENT=1 CONF_NRPE=1
CONF_NSCA=1 CONF_CHECKS=1 CONF_NSCLIENT=1 CONF_SCHEDULER=1
CONF_CAN_CHANGE=1 MONITORING_TOOL=none NSCLIENT_PWD="N@g10sP@55w0rd"
        wait: true

    - name: Copying NSClient personalised configuration
      file
      win_copy:
        src: ~/win_apps/conf_files/nsclient.ini
```

```
      dest: C:\Program Files\NSClient++\nsclient.ini

  - name: Change execution policy to allow the NSClient script remote
Nagios execution
    raw: Start-Process powershell -verb RunAs -ArgumentList 'Set-
ExecutionPolicy RemoteSigned -Force'

  - name: Restart the NSclient service to apply the
    configuration change
    win_service:
      name: nscp
      start_mode: auto
      state: restarted

  - name: Delete the MSI file
    win_file: path=C:\NSCP-0.5.0.62-x64.msi state=absent
```

This playbook can be applied to a large number of applications that can be installed using an MSI file.

Network automation

Just like computers, Ansible can be used to automate the management of network devices if they run some kind of remote service, preferably SSH. In this section, we are going to explore some use cases on CISCO network devices. We will look at various tasks that are time-consuming when done manually.

Use case 1 – automated patching of network devices

We are going to follow the recommended method for upgrading a network device. We need to make sure that we back up both the running and startup configuration. We will then start patching one device at a time using the serial option:

```
---
- name: Patch CISCO network devices
  hosts: ciscoswitches
  remote_user: admin
  strategy: debug
  connection: ssh
  serial: 1
  gather_facts: yes
```

```
tasks:
  - name: Backup the running-config and the startup-
    config to the local machine
    ntc_save_config:
        local_file: "images/{{ inventory_hostname
        }}.cfg"
        platform: 'cisco_ios_ssh'
        username: admin
        password: "P@55w0rd"
        secret: "5ecretP@55"
        host: "{{ inventory_hostname }}"

  - name: Upload binary file to the CISCO devices
    ntc_file_copy:
        local_file: " images/ios.bin'"
        remote_file: 'cXXXX-adventerprisek9sna.bin'
        platform: 'cisco_ios_ssh'
        username: admin
        password: "P@55w0rd"
        secret: "5ecretP@55"
        host: "{{ inventory_hostname }}"

  - name: Reload CISCO device to apply new patch
    ios_command:
        commands:
          - "reload in 5\ny"
        platform: 'cisco_ios_ssh'
        username: admin
        password: "P@55w0rd"
        secret: "5ecretP@55"
        host: "{{ inventory_hostname }}"
```

You can create a fact variable called `provider` that has all the credentials and information about the device to be used for running commands. Defining the variables minimizes the amount of code that can be put in a playbook.

Use case 2 – adding a new configuration in network devices

In this use case, we are going to change some of the generic configurations on Cisco devices. We are going to change the hostname, create a banner, upgrade the SSH to version 2, change the Cisco VTP mode, and configure the DNS server and the NTP server:

```
---
```

```
- name: Patch CISCO network devices
  hosts: ciscoswitches
  become: yes
  become_method: enable
  ansible_connection: network_cli
  ansible_ssh_pass=admin
  ansible_become_pass="P@55w0rd"
  ansible_network_os=ios
  strategy: debug
  connection: ssh
  serial: 1
  gather_facts: yes
  tasks:
    - name: Update network device hostname to match the
      one used in the inventory
      ios_config:
          authorize: yes
          lines: ['hostname {{ inventory_hostname }}']
          force: yes

    - name: Change the CISCO devices login banner
      ios_config:
          authorize: yes
          lines:
              - banner motd ^This device is controlled via
                Ansible. Please refrain from doing any
                manual modification^

    - name: upgrade SSh service to version2
      ios_config:
          authorize: yes
          lines:
              - ip ssh version 2

    - name: Configure VTP to use transparent mode
      ios_config:
          authorize: yes
          lines:
              - vtp mode transparent

    - name: Change DNS servers to point to the Google DNS
      ios_config:
          authorize: yes
          lines:
              - ip name-server 8.8.8.8
              - ip name-server 8.8.4.4

    - name: Configure some realisable NTP servers
```

```
ios_config:
   authorize: yes
   lines:
      - ntp server time.nist.gov
      - ntp server 0.uk.pool.ntp.org
```

It is recommended that you use these playbooks during downtime or in a planned maintenance window. A configuration might go wrong for one device but work perfectly fine with others. The Ansible summary always has a detailed execution status that tracks down problematic devices and tasks.

Automation of the cloud and container infrastructure

This section is more relevant to resource management than to the hosts themselves. Any of the preceding use cases can be used for either bare metal or virtual hosts that are located locally or on the cloud.

The wake-on-LAN modules are less useful in a cloud or virtual environment. It is easier to manage virtual hosts and instances using the dedicated modules for their controllers.

VMware automation

In this subsection, we will look at some use cases for host management in a VMware environment, including managing the infrastructure around them.

Use case 1 – creating virtual machines from a template

This use case shows how to create virtual machines from a predefined template. After that, we make sure that all the VMs have been added to the inventory with the right parameters:

```
---
- name: Create a virtual machine from a template
  hosts: localhost
  gather_facts: False
  tasks:
    - name: Create a virtual machine
```

```
        vmware_guest:
          hostname: 'vcenter.edu.lab'
          username: 'vmadmin@lab.edu'
          password: 'VMp@55w0rd'
          datecenter: 'vcenter.edu.lab'
          validate_certs: no
          esxi_hostname: 'esxi1.lab.edu'
          template: ubuntu1404Temp
          folder: '/DeployedVMs'
          name: '{{ item.hostname }}'
          state: poweredon
          disk:
            - size_gb: 50
              type: thin
              datastore: 'datastore1'
          networks:
            - name: 'LabNetwork'
              ip: '{{ item.ip }}'
              netmask: '255.255.255.0'
              gateway: '192.168.13.1'
              dns_servers:
                - '8.8.8.8'
                - '8.8.4.4'
          hardware:
              memory_mb: '1024'
              num_cpus: '2'
          wait_for_ip_address: yes
        delegate_to: localhost
        with_items:
            - { hostname: vm1, ip: 192.168.13.10 }
            - { hostname: vm2, ip: 192.168.13.11 }
            - { hostname: vm3, ip: 192.168.13.12 }

    - name: add newly created VMs to the Ansible
      inventory
      add_host:
        hostname: "{{ item.hostname }}"
        ansible_host: "{{ item.ip }}"
        ansible_ssh_user: setup
        ansible_ssh_pass: "L1nuxP@55w0rd"
        ansible_connection: ssh
        groupname: Linux
      with_items:
          - { hostname: vm1, ip: 192.168.13.10 }
          - { hostname: vm2, ip: 192.168.13.11 }
          - { hostname: vm3, ip: 192.168.13.12 }
```

The use of items in this playbook can be altered by using the predefined variables.

Use case 2 – ESXi hosts and cluster management

We will now try to carry out some higher-level infrastructure management. We will try to create a VMware cluster and add an ESXi host to it:

```
---
- name: Create a VMware cluster and populate it
  hosts: localhost
  gather_facts: False
  tasks:
    - name: Create a VMware virtual cluster
      vmware_cluster:
          hostname: 'vcenter.edu.lab'
          username: 'vmadmin@lab.edu'
          password: 'VMp@55w0rd'
          datecenter: 'vcenter.edu.lab'
          validate_certs: no
          cluster_name: "LabCluster"
          state: present
          enable_ha: yes
          enable_drs: yes
          enable_vsan: no

    - name: Add a VMware ESXi host to the newly created
      Cluster
      vmware_host:
          hostname: 'vcenter.edu.lab'
          username: 'vmadmin@lab.edu'
          password: 'VMp@55w0rd'
          datecenter: 'vcenter.edu.lab'
          validate_certs: no
          cluster_name: " LabCluster "
          esxi_hostname: "esxi1.lab.edu"
          esxi_username: "root"
          esxi_password: "E5X1P@55w0rd"
          state: present
```

These playbooks can replace both the PowerCLI commands that are used to manage the VCenter and the manual process of accessing the Windows client or the web interface to manage hosts and clusters.

Summary

In this chapter, we covered many interesting use cases that any system administrator will need to run at some point. Many other tasks can be performed, like we did with customized playbooks. But not every script is considered to be a good automation; what matters is that the right nodes go from state A to state B with no errors and in less time. In Chapter 6, *Ansible Coding for Configuration Management*, we are going to learn some advanced script optimization techniques based on best practices in order to get the best out of Ansible automation.

References

Ansible documentation: `https://docs.ansible.com/ansible/latest/`

Ansible GitHub project: `https://github.com/ansible`

Chocolatey packages index: `https://chocolatey.org/packages`

6

Ansible Coding for Configuration Management

The main way in which you'll learn Ansible coding is by writing your own Ansible playbooks, either for fun or to solve your own infrastructure challenges. However, at a certain point, things may start to get complicated. Your code might be working, but how do you know if it is really doing the task in the right way? Is it efficient? How scalable will it be? Using meaningful names makes it easier to understand your code. Issues may also arise to do with script organization: it is easy to end up with a folder filled with several scripts, even if they have nothing to do with each other.

In this chapter, we're going to talk about the standards and best practices for writing Ansible playbooks. We are aiming to improve our playbooks by speeding up tasks, improving security, providing accommodation for built-in infrastructure redundancy systems, optimizing their tasks, and reducing code repetition to produce smaller playbooks with the same functionality. Finally, we are going to introduce Ansible roles, which are the ultimate task optimization tool in Ansible.

This chapter will cover the following topics:

- Standards for writing playbooks in Ansible
- Best practices when coding YAML playbooks
- Optimizing Ansible tasks and playbooks
- Ansible roles
- Examples with Ansible roles

Ansible configuration management coding standards

In this section, we are going to list several rules and methods to help with writing nice and clean playbooks in conformity with the Ansible norm. This is not a strict instruction to follow, but instead a representation of how Ansible developers and maintainers think it should be used. Following these norms does not just allow easier usage of playbooks, it also helps make it standard and understandable by the community members, therefore enabling better team collaboration.

 These standards are based on the experience of Ansible users and maintainers. Any individual user may use Ansible differently, in a way that would require a different set of rules.

Playbook and task naming

When making a playbook, using the `name:` field is optional. If you write a playbook with no name, it will work perfectly fine. The following is an example of a playbook that does not have a name:

```
---
- hosts: servers
  become: yes
  gather_facts: false
  tasks:
    - apt: update_cache=yes
    - apt:
        name: mc
    - file:
        path: /usr/local/projects
        mode: 1777
        state: directory
```

This playbook may have an output that looks as follows:

```
)alibi@alibi-ml ~/vagrant-ansible-lab> ansible-playbook playbooks/sample-playbook.yml

PLAY [servers] *************************************************************

TASK [apt] *****************************************************************
changed: [server2]
changed: [server0]
changed: [server1]

TASK [apt] *****************************************************************
changed: [server2]
changed: [server1]
changed: [server0]

TASK [file] ****************************************************************
changed: [server1]
changed: [server2]
changed: [server0]

PLAY RECAP ****************************************************************
server0                    : ok=3    changed=3    unreachable=0    failed=0
server1                    : ok=3    changed=3    unreachable=0    failed=0
server2                    : ok=3    changed=3    unreachable=0    failed=0
```

The playbook has done what we have asked it to do, but the fact that it doesn't have a name may present a problem if we have many tasks in one playbook because we won't be able to monitor the status of each job as easily. Following Ansible's standards, writing a playbook that has a better description of each of its tasks can help a lot. The benefits of having a clear description of tasks helps with personal or team task monitoring, providing a better explanation of its pipelines for co-workers and community users. An example of a more descriptive playbook might look as follows:

```
---
- name: Setup users projects workspace with a file manager
  hosts: servers
  become: yes
  gather_facts: false
  tasks:
    - name: Update Package manager repo index
      apt: update_cache=yes
    - name: Install Midnight commander as a terminal file manager
      apt:
```

```
    name: mc
  - name: Create the projects workspace folder with sticky bit
    file:
    path: /usr/local/projects
    mode: 1777
    state: directory
```

This way, we get a more descriptive output:

```
alibi@alibi-ml ~/vagrant-ansible-lab> ansible-playbook playbooks/sample-playbook.yml

PLAY [Setup users projects workspace with a file manager] ****************************

TASK [Update Pakcage manager repo index] ********************************************
changed: [server1]
changed: [server2]
changed: [server0]

TASK [Install Midnight Commander as a terminal file manager] ************************
ok: [server0]
ok: [server2]
ok: [server1]

TASK [Create the projects workspace folder with sticky bit] *************************
changed: [server1]
changed: [server2]
changed: [server0]

PLAY RECAP *************************************************************************
server0                  : ok=3    changed=2    unreachable=0    failed=0
server1                  : ok=3    changed=2    unreachable=0    failed=0
server2                  : ok=3    changed=2    unreachable=0    failed=0
```

It is up to you to decide what to write and which aspects of the tasks are described, as long as it makes sense to the user, either yourself, your team, or the community. We recommend simply phrased sentences that explain the tasks briefly.

YAML syntax usage for playbooks

Since playbooks are written in YAML, you have a bit of wiggle room regarding what the code looks like when introducing task arguments. Again, although Ansible will accept the code and the task will be executed, it is easy to end up with long lines of code for an averagely complicated task. This is what a one-line Ansible task looks like:

```
- name: Copy user configuration
copy: src=/home/admin/setup.conf dest=/usr/local/projects/ owner=setup
group=dev mode=0677 backup=yes
```

Instead of this, we can follow a neat and more organized YAML structure, by adding white spaces in front of each task argument. The playbook should look as follows:

```
 - name: Copy user configuration
copy:
src: /home/admin/setup.conf
dest: /usr/local/projects/
owner: setup
group: dev
mode: 0677
backup: yes
```

However, some tasks or commands may have long strings, either the absolute path of a file or a long piece of text to be used for a task. Ansible does offer a way of organizing tasks with long strings using the > character to write a single-line string in multiple lines without carrying the returns:

```
- name: Fill in sample text file
  lineinfile:
    path: /usr/local/projects/setup.conf
    line: >
        This is the configuration file for the user
        Setup. Please do not edit make any change
        to it if you are not and administrator.
```

> Ansible offers an option to check the syntax of a playbook to see whether it is conforming with YAML syntax. To use this, add the --syntax-check option to the Ansible command.

The become feature

Many tasks need to be executed by a specific user, either to access restricted resources or to enable user-specific services. Although there are some Shell or Powershell commands that allow this, they may produce very long and complicated commands. The Ansible become or become_user feature allows for easier tasks that are personalized for each specific user. This feature is considered as a standard for Ansible configuration management coding owing to the level of task optimization that is offered by Ansible to simplify complicated commands, making this feature not just playbook-personalized but also task specific. The following is an example of a playbook that uses this feature:

```
---
- name: Organize users projects folders
  hosts: servers
  become: yes
  remote_user: setup
  gather_facts: false
  tasks:
    - name: create folder for user1
      command: mkdir /usr/local/projects/user1
       become_user: user1
   - name: Create test space for setup
      file:
       path: /usr/local/projects/setup/test
       mode: 1777
       state: directory
---
```

Group organization

Host group organization makes it possible to organize hosts in groups based on role, geographical location, or data center location. In a parent and child structure, it is possible to set parent group variables and make the child group inherit them. To override parent group variables, individual hosts or child groups can have their own unique custom variables. This practice is more of an Ansible inventory management feature than for playbook coding, yet it is very important for multi-architecture configuration management.

As described in previous chapters, host variables can either be defined within the inventory or the playbook itself. But it is easier to manage when organized within the inventory files as group_vars and hosts_vars.

The following example for an inventory file shows how parent and child group variables can be defined:

```
/etc/ansible/hosts:
[linuxservers:children]
webservers
loadbalancers

[linuxservers:vars]
remote_user: setup
ntpserver: 0.uk.pool.ntp.org
become: yes

[webservers]
node0
```

```
node1
node2

[webservers:vars]
remote_user: devadmin
ansible_connection: ssh

[loadbalancers]
node3
node4

[loadbalancers:vars]
ntpserver: 0.us.pool.ntp.org
ansible_connection: docker
```

This is not the only structure that can be used to define groups. The inventory file can only hold the structure of the groups, and then each group can have their own inventory file that holds their variables. The same rule applies where a child variable overrides a parent variable.

Using handlers

Ansible recommends using handlers for task pipelining, as handlers are programmed tasks that are executed when they are notified. Handlers will be fired for tasks which report a changed state. They are often used for service management following a configuration change. This ensures fluid configuration management as whenever changes happen in the host, the services involved should be restarted to apply the change.

Ansible also has a feature to enable the mass flushing of handlers in playbooks. This feature allows you to control when the changes can be applied by controlling the execution of all handlers in a task. Using meta, task handlers can be flushed from any position in the playbook:

```
---
- name: Change service settings and apply it
  hosts: servers
  become: yes
  remote_user: setup
  gather_facts: false
  tasks:
    - name: Flush the playbook handlers
      meta: flush_handlers

    - name: Change ntp service config
      lineinfile:
```

```
        path: /etc/ntp.conf
        line: "server 0.us.pool.ntp.org"

    - name: Flush the playbook handlers
      meta: flush_handlers

  handlers:
    - name: restart ntp service
      service:
        name: ntp
        state: restarted
```

Password usage in playbooks

Many tasks require you to input a password to access a database or to use a CLI or access a third-party Terminal. It is never advisable to write passwords or other sensitive information openly on a playbook. There are multiple ways to protect this information. The two most common examples are to store them in another protected playbook or to use Ansible Vault.

In this section, we will mainly cover storing passwords and sensitive variables in other, more protected files. Ansible Vault will be covered thoroughly in a later chapter.

The idea is to create a playbook that contains several sensitive variables and store it in a secure location with restricted permissions. Then, the playbook calls for its variable using the `include` option at the play level (where the tasks are located):

```
---
- name: usage of sensative variable
  hosts: servers
  include: passwords_playbook.yml
  tasks:
    - name: add a MySQL user
      mysql_user:
        name: user1
        password: {{ mysql_user1_password }}
        priv: '*.*:ALL'
        state: present
```

This method is very easy to use and manage, but it is not the best in terms of security. Ansible Vault will provide better protection for sensitive information in playbooks.

Ansible Vault is not the only tool that allows you to secure variables in Ansible. There are other third-party tools that allow you to secure passwords and critical information by preventing them from being typed as clear text.

Playbook version control

It is highly recommended to use a version control service, such as GitHub, SubVersion, or Mercurial, to manage your Ansible playbooks. Besides the countless benefits of using version control for any coding, Ansible playbooks can use GitHub projects as an input to enable frameworks that allow continuous deployment and integration. By updating your code in the repository, it gets updated on all the systems it is used in.

Making Ansible roles where possible

The best way to optimize a task is to make it an Ansible role, or preferably multiple roles if it has multiple goals. A task that has been transformed into a role is ready to be used with multiple situations, and it can be shared to be used by other users. Roles can be included in multiple playbooks to avoid writing the same lines of code twice or more. Ansible has a role-sharing platform called Galaxy, where the community shares their roles with other users. We will cover this in more detail in the next chapter.

Ansible coding best practices

After exploring the standards that should be followed by Ansible developers, let's now have a look at what Ansible daily users recommend as best practice for good configuration management using Ansible.

These methods may suit some setups more than others. Not every method is a good option for your environment; they may cause more trouble than benefits if they are applied inappropriately. We have collected the methods that we believe are common and useful most of the time.

Using comments in playbooks

Earlier in this chapter, we discussed naming plays or tasks in the playbook to provide a better description for the reader. However, when performing unusual tasks or running commands that form part of a bigger picture, having a descriptive name is not always enough information.

You can use comments either at the start of each playbook, explaining its overall role, or in the pipelines included within the playbook. You can also offer some information about the author, including contact details when the playbook gets shared within the community. Having comments in the code you write is a good idea for any coding you do, especially if you are planning to share it. It makes any script user-friendly. Even though YAML is an easy coding language, it is not always obvious when reading the work of others. This example playbook shows a way to get more detailed information about a playbook:

```
---
#######################################
#
# This playbook with a goal to achieve number of tasks in a pipeline
# to configure several Linux hosts for collaborative projects. It starts by
# setting up the needed tools and services, then configure them to a
# standard, then prepared the shared space, and assign the users and
groups.
#
# Author: ***** ***** email: ********@****
#
#######################################
- name: Hosts provisioning playbook
  hosts: linuxservers
  become: yes
  remote_user: setup
  gather_facts: false
  tasks:
    - name: Install Midnight commander
      # This is a terminal based file manager does not require a GUI
interface
      apt:
       name: mc
  ...
```

Playbook files and folder naming

This is a best practice that should be followed in life, not just for scripting and playbooks! Whenever you create a file in your computer, on the cloud, or within an application, always make sure to give it a name that reveals what it is. You can also organize your files into subfolders with descriptive names. Although it might take longer for a user to navigate through the folders to get to the playbook, everything will be well explained and clear.

Avoiding the use of command modules

Ansible offers a few modules that allow you to run commands to be executed as they are in the remote hosts. This is handy when the Ansible modules do not cover the task that is intended to be performed, which is especially the case when there are complex tasks.

The issue with command modules is that they do not know whether the task has been properly executed since they can execute any command running any tool, service, and system. The return values for a command can easily be misunderstood and sometimes do not reflect what really happened after the command execution. It is recommended that you use the `changed_when` option in the task in the playbook, so it looks as follows:

```
    - name: Execute a Windows Write Filter enabling command and identify if
it made change
      win_shell: ewfm.exe -conf enable
      register: output
      changed_when: "output.stdout == 'Awaiting for next boot to apply the
change.'"
```

There are multiple methods for collecting command changes; this is one of the ones that was most recommended in the community. File and service status modules can be used to check changes in the data via tasks or handlers, but these may cause extra tasks to be sent to the remote hosts.

Avoiding ignoring module errors

Ansible offers the option of ignoring some task errors when they are reported. This is because Ansible by default halts a playbook if one of its tasks has failed. Sometimes, if a task is used to execute an optional job or to test a particular aspect of the system, the task isn't important enough to cause the entire playbook to halt. We tend to add the `ignore_errors: yes` option at the end of these tasks, but this is a very bad habit that may cause damage to your hosts, especially in pipelined tasks.

The best way to deal with optional tasks or those that return an error even when they have executed what is needed is to use the `failed_when` and `changed_when` options to define when a task has failed or performed its job.

Using Ansible conditions

We can use the information collected by Ansible about the hosts it manages to personalize tasks to a specific system using Ansible conditions. Not all modules work with every OS. To make a playbook universal, we can add in some settings where some tasks test the facts of the remote host before executing the task. This also helps with reducing the number of playbook scripts by creating scripts that adapt themselves to the system that they are being executed on. As an example, let's try to install the same package with two different names in Debian and Red Hat Linux OS:

```
---
- name: Install python development package on Linux hosts
  hosts: linuxservers
  become: yes
  remote_user: setup
  gather_facts: true
  tasks:
    - name: install python development on Debian systems
      apt:
          name: python-dev
      when: ansible_os_family == "Debian"

    - name: install python development on Red Hat systems
      yum:
          name: python-devel
      when: ansible_os_family == "RedHat"
```

Using Ansible loops

Ansible loops offer several possibilities. One of the most common uses is to reduce the amount of code when running the same module multiple times on different inputs. The idea is to define a variable or an object variable that has its own variables, then populate the list with the different entries.

The following playbook shows a good use of Ansible loops to copy several configuration files with different sources, destinations, and ACL settings:

```
---
- name: Copy users config files to their project directory
```

```
hosts: linuxservers
become: yes
remote_user: setup
gather_facts: true
tasks:
  - name: Copy user config files
    copy:
        src: '{{ item.src }}'
        dest: '{{ item.dest }}'
        mode: '{{ item.mode | default("0744") }}'
        owner: '{{ item.owner | default("nobody") }}'
    when_items:
    - { src: "/media/share/config/user1.conf",
        dest: "/usr/local/projetsfolder/user1",
        mode: "0774", owner: "user1" }}
      - { src: "/media/share/config/user2.conf",
          dest: "/usr/local/projetsfolder/user2",
          mode: "0700", owner: "user2" }}
      - { src: "/media/share/samples/users.conf",
          dest: "/usr/local/projetsfolder/", mode: "0777" }}
```

 The default option takes cares of empty entries by replacing them with what has been entered as the default value.

Using template files

It is recommended that you use modules that edit configuration files, such as `lineinfile` or `blockinfile`. These can help significantly with setting up standard configurations or updating old settings. However, when these files are automated, they cannot handle the small changes that can be identified easily when modifying manually, leading to unpredictable changes. There is no simple way of telling whether a configuration change will go as expected, especially for a large infrastructure. For this reason, it is recommended to use template files to act as base configuration files, scripts, or web pages. Still, we can use `lineinfile` or `blockinfile` as a backup plan. In these, the user knows exactly what to set up, what to edit, and what to leave for each host. This method helps to control the unpredictability of tasks.

Using the `template` module, we can generate configuration files that are specific to the hosts from a `Jinja` file. The example `.j2` template file gets filled in with predefined variables, as follows:

```
db.conf.j2:
```

```
mysql_db_hosts = '{{ db_serv_hostname }}'
mysql_db_name = '{{ db_name }}'
mysql_db_user = '{{ db_username }}'
mysql_db_pass = '{{ db_password }}'
```

These variables can then be defined in the same playbook or another YAML file, included at the play level:

```
---
- name: Copy Database configuration file
  hosts: linux    servers
  become: yes
  remote_user: setup
  gather_facts: true
  tasks:
    - name: Import variable from an other YAML
      include_vars: /home/admin/variables/database2.yml
    - name: Copy db config file
      template:
          src: /home/admin/template/db.conf.j2
          dest: /etc/mysql/db.conf
          owner: bin
          group: wheel
          mode: 0600
```

> The Jinja2 files offer a level of control over the variable structure. You can introduce loops and conditional statements with some predefined functions to alter the input to match the structure of the configuration file input.

Stating task status

When creating files, setting up configuration, or managing services, an Ansible user should always state the status of the object of the task, even when the change is aimed at its default value. Even though this will add an extra line to most of your tasks, it is a good habit to have. It is one of those practices that some people think is useless, but for debugging purposes, or for anyone reading your script, seeing the status of each task provides a better view of what each task has done. Naming the task indicates what you want it to do, but it does not necessarily mean that the task has done that action. Using the state option, however, gives a much clearer indication in this respect:

```
tasks:
  - name: create a new file
    file:
        path: /usr/local/projects/vars.txt
```

```
        state: present

    - name: removing line to a file
      lineinfile:
          path: /usr/local/projects/conf.txt
          line: "adminuser = user0"
          state: absent
```

Shared storage space for data tasks

The Ansible management server is doing a lot more in the background than simply sending tasks and managing remote machines. Adding the extra task of managing file transfers and running them on its interface may cause a considerable performance degradation. We always recommend using shared storage space either on an FTP server, an NFS or Samba filesystem, or on a web server to be downloaded by the remote hosts. This practice ensures that the remote hosts carry out the transfer with another dedicated and optimized server.

It is always a good practice to have all tools archived and their sample configuration files stored in a network file system. Remote hosts can easily access the drives either temporarily for a data transfer or permanently if they are in constant need.

The following playbook task shows an example of the code for this use:

```
    tasks:
      - name: Copy a tool archive to remote host
        copy:
            src: /media/nfshsare/Tools/tool1.tar.gz
            dest: /usr/local/tools/
            mode: 0755
```

Ansible roles

This is the section in which we discover Ansible roles and what we can do with them to optimize our automation scripting.

What are Ansible roles?

The ultimate configuration management scripts optimization is to convert simple playbooks into Ansible roles. This gives you the ability to make a set of configuration management tasks modular and reusable, with multiple configurations. It also means that they can be easily shared when required. Ansible roles allow several related tasks, with their variables and dependencies, to be contained in a portable framework. This framework represents the breakdown of a complex playbook into multiple simple files.

An Ansible role is composed of multiple folders, each of which contain several YAML files. By default, they have a `main.yml` file, but they can have more than one when needed. This is a standardized structure for all Ansible roles, which allows Ansible playbooks to automatically load predefined variables, tasks, handlers, templates, and default values located in separate YAML files. Each Ansible role should contain at least one of the following directories, if not all of them.

The tasks folder

This is the controller folder. It contains the main YAML files. The code within those files executes the main role tasks by calling all the other defined elements of the role. Usually, it has the `main.yml` file with some YAML files that are OS-specific that ensure certain tasks are executed when the role is run on specific systems. It may also contain other tasks to set up, configure, or ensure the existence of certain tools, services, configuration folders, or packages that failed a test run by the main script and triggered the execution of a task to fix them. The following is a sample task code written on the `main.yml` file in the `tasks` folder:

```
tasks/main.yml:
---
    - name: check if NTP is installed
      stat:
          path: /etc/init.d/ntpd
      register: tool_status

    - include_tasks: debian.yml
      when: tool_status.stat.exists

    - name: Copy the NTP config to remote host
      template:
          src: /template/ntp.conf.j2
          dest: /etc/ntpd/ntpd.conf
          mode: 0400
      notify:
          - Restart ntp
```

```
tasks/debian.yml:
---
    - name: Copy a NTP config to remote host
      apt:
          name: ntp
          state: latest
```

The handlers folder

This folder usually contains the main file with multiple handler tasks that are waiting to be triggered by other tasks, either with the role or from other playbooks or roles. It is mainly used for service management to apply a configuration change performed by another task. Here is an example of a handler script:

```
handlers/main.yml:
---
    - name: Restart ntp
      service:
          name: ntp
          state: restarted
```

The vars folder

This is where the role variables get stored. Usually, it is used for a permanent variable that does not require any changes between environments. Here is an example of a variables file:

```
vars/main.yml:
---
ntpserv1: 0.uk.pool.ntp.org
ntpserv2: 1.uk.pool.ntp.org
```

The templates folder

This folder contains the template files used by the role to create the actual configuration files. These are then deployed by the role to the remote hosts. They are `Jinja2` template engine scripts that enable loops and other features. Here is an example of a template file:

```
template/ntp.conf.j2:
driftfile /var/lib/ntp/ntp.drift
filegen loopstats file loopstats type day enable
filegen peerstats file peerstats type day enable
filegen clockstats file clockstats type day enable

loop {{ ntpserv1 }}
```

```
loop {{ ntpserv2 }}

pool ntp.ubuntu.com
restrict -4 default kod notrap nomodify nopeer noquery limited
restrict -6 default kod notrap nomodify nopeer noquery limited
restrict 127.0.0.1
restrict ::1
restrict source notrap nomodify noquery
```

The defaults folder

This folder contains the default values for the non-defined variables in the role when they are used. It is a way of organizing variable inputs in the role and is one of the highly recommended options when writing a playbook. It allows for a centralized management of the default values of the variable of the role. Default values are always vulnerable because they change a lot depending on the needs and policies of the user. Having this solution allows one file to change all the values. Here is an example of a `defaults` folder:

```
` ` `
defaults/main.yml:
---
timout: 2000
ID_key: "None"
` ` `
```

The files folder

This folder holds all extra files that are required to achieve the role task. These files usually get dispatched to remote hosts as part of certain tasks. They are usually static, and they do not contain any variables to change, be copied, extracted, or compressed to the remote host.

The meta folder

This folder contains machine-readable information about the role. These folders contain the role metadata, which includes information about authors, licenses, compatibilities, and dependencies. The main use for this option is to declare dependencies, more specifically, roles. If the current role relies on another role, that gets declared in a `meta` folder. The following example shows how `meta` folders are used:

```
` ` `
meta/main.yml:
---
```

```
galaxy_info:
  author: medalibi
  description: NTP client installn
  company: Packt
  license: license (GPLv3, BSD)
  min_ansible_version: 2.4
  platforms:
    - name: Ubuntu
      version:
        - 16.04
        - 18.04
  galaxy_tags:
    - networking
    - system

dependencies: []
```

The test folder

This folder contains a test environment with an inventory file and a playbook script to test the role. It is usually used by the developers to test any new changes that have happened to the role. It also serves as a sample configuration for new users to follow the running of the role. The playbook script within the test folder looks as follows:

```
tests/test.yml:
---
- hosts: servers
  remote_user: setup
  become: yes
  roles:
    - ntpclient.lab.edu
```

The README folder/file

This is a folder that can be replaced by a simple markdown README.md file. It is an optional feature but it is highly recommended when you are planning to share your roles. It acts as a documentation for the role: it can contain anything that might be useful for first-time users of the role from a simple description of the task delivered by the role, to instructions and requirements to set up this role on their environment. It might also contain some best practices and information about the author and contributors if it is built by a team.

Ansible roles are used for replacing the same function that the option `include` carry out when adding extra parameters and functions to a playbook. Roles are much more organized and allow easier sharing, either on a personal GitHub project or on the Ansible Galaxy. This will be our subject for the next chapter.

Make sure to use descriptive names for your roles. Like playbooks, this helps the users of your role to have an idea of what your role should do. Your description should be brief, usually just one or two words. You can always add more detail and description in the README file.

Roles tend to be very specific: they do one job and one job only. It is not advisable to have tasks within a role that have nothing to do with the job. Let's create some example Ansible roles that deliver a few jobs to use as template roles that follow all best practices.

Creating Ansible roles

Let's now create an Ansible role from scratch. This role is a Samba file server setup on either of the big families of Linux. It serves a folder that is accessible via a shared user.

First, let's create our role folder using the `ansible-galaxy` command line. Before running the command, we need to change the Terminal workspace to the location in which we would like to store our Ansible roles:

```
cd ~/Roles/
ansible-galaxy init samba.lab.edu
```

We should see the following output:

```
- samba.lab.edu was created successfully
```

We then create a folder with the name of the role, with the following structure of subfolders and files:

```
samba.lab.edu
└── README.md
├── defaults
│   └── main.yml
├── files
│
├── handlers
│   └── main.yml
├── meta
│   └── main.yml
```

```
├──── tasks
│     └──── main.yml
├──── templates
│
├──── tests
│     ├──── inventory
│     └──── test.yml
└──── vars
      └──── main.yml
```

Let's now populate our folder and files with the appropriate code for the role. First, we are going to populate the dependencies and requirements for the role to work. For this, we will be working on the meta, template, files, vars, and defaults folders, and the OS-specific scripts in the tasks folder.

We will start by populating the template folder with a Jinga2 template file for the configuration of the SMB service:

```
template/smb.conf.j2:
#========= Global Settings =========
# Samba server configuration:
[global]
  workgroup = {{ wrk_grp | upper }} ## upper convert any input to uppercase.
  server string = Samba Server %v
  netbios name = {{ os_name }}
  security = user
map to guest = bad user
dns proxy = no

#========= Share Definitions =========
# Samba shared folder:
[{{ smb_share_name }}]
  path = {{ smb_share_path }}
  valid users = @{{ smb_grp }}
  guest ok = no
  read only = no
  browsable =yes
  writable = yes
  force user = nobody
  create mask = {{ add_mod }}
  directory mask = {{ dir_mod }}
```

We are then going to put a text file in the files folder that contains the rules and policies of using the shared folder:

```
files/Fileserver_rules.txt:
This shared drive is to be used by designated teams.
```

```
Any distractive usage will cause a follow up on the incident.
Please do not change any of your team members folders or delete anything
you are not assigned to manage.

For any inquiries please contact admin@edu.lab
```

After that, we edit the main file in the `meta` folder with some role information: author, description, support, and tags. This will look as follows:

```
meta/main.yml
---
dependencies: []

galaxy_info:
  author: medalibi
  description: "Samba server setup and configuration on Linux OS
(Debian/Red Hat)"
  license: "license (GPLv3, BSD)"
  min_ansible_version: 2.5
  platforms:
    - name: Debian
      versions:
      - 8
      - 9
    - name: Ubuntu
      versions:
      - 14.04
      - 16.04
      - 18.04
    - name: EL
      versions:
        - 6
        - 7

  galaxy_tags:
    - system
    - networking
    - fileserver
    - windows
```

Once this is done, we move on to defining the role variables. For this role, we are going to have all the variables stored in one file, including the OS-specific variable:

```
vars/main.yml
---
debian_smb_pkgs:
    - samba
    - samba-client
```

```
  - samba-common
  - python-glade2
  - system-config-samba

redhat_smb_pkgs:
  - samba
  - samba-client
  - samba-common
  - cifs-utils


smb_selinux_pkg:
  - libsemanage-python

smb_selinux_bln:
  - samba_enable_home_dirs
  - samba_export_all_rw

samba_config_path: /etc/samba/smb.conf

debian_smb_services:
  - smbd
  - nmbd

redhat_smb_services:
  - smb
  - nmb
```

To set our default values, we fill in the defaults main folder with the following file:

```
defaults/main.yml:
---
wrk_grp: WORKGROUP
os_name: debian
smb_share_name: SharedWorkspace
smb_share_path: /usr/local/share
add_mod: 0700
dir_mod: 0700

smb_grp: smbgrp
smb_user: 'shareduser1'
smb_pass: '5h@redP@55w0rd'
```

We now create the OS-specific tasks for setting up the service:

```
tasks/Debian_OS.yml:
---
- name: Install Samba packages on Debian family Linux
```

```
    apt:
      name: "{{ item }}"
      state: latest
      update_cache: yes
    with_items: "{{ debian_smb_pkgs }}"


  tasks/RedHat_OS.yml:
  ---
  - name: Install Samba packages on Red Hat family Linux
    yum:
      name: "{{ item }}"
      state: latest
      update_cache: yes
    with_items: "{{ redhat_smb_pkgs }}"

  - name: Install SELinux packages for Red Hat
    yum:
      name: "{{ item }}"
      state: present
    with_items: "{{ smb_selinux_pkg }}"

  - name: Configure Red Hat SELinux Boolean
    seboolean:
      name: "{{ item }}"
      state: true
      persistent: true
    with_items: "{{ smb_selinux_bln }}"
```

Let's now finish by adding the main task and the handlers for it:

```
  tasks/main.yml:
  ---
  - name: Setup Samba based on host OS
    include_tasks: "{{ ansible_os_family }}_OS.yml"

  - name: Create the Samba share access group
    group:
      name: "{{ smb_grp }}"
      state: present

  - name: Create the Samba access user
    user:
      name: "{{ smb_user }}"
      groups: "{{ smb_grp }}"
      append: yes
  - name: Define the user password within Samba
      shell: "(echo {{ smb_pass }}; echo {{ smb_pass }}) |
```

```
        smbpasswd -s -a {{ smb_user }}"

  - name: Check that the shared directory exist
    stat:
      path: "{{ smb_share_path }}"
    register: share_dir

  - name: Make sure the shared directory is present
    file:
      state: directory
      path: "{{ smb_share_path }}"
      owner: "{{ smb_user }}"
      group: "{{ smb_grp }}"
      mode: '0777'
      recurse: yes
    when: share_dir.stat.exists == False

  - name: Deploy the Samba configuration file
    template:
      dest: "{{ samba_config_path }}"
      src: smb.conf.j2
      validate: 'testparm -s %s'
      backup: yes
    notify:
      - Restart Samba

  - name: Enable and start Samba services on Debian family
    service:
      name: "{{ item }}"
      state: started
      enabled: true
    with_items: "{{ debian_smb_services }}"
    when: ansible_os_family == 'Debian'

  - name: Enable and start Samba services on RedHat family
    service:
      name: "{{ item }}"
      state: started
      enabled: true
    with_items: "{{ redhat_smb_services }}"
    when: ansible_os_family == 'RedHat'
```

We finish by defining the handlers for service management:

```
/handlers/main.yml:
---
- name: Restart Samba
  service:
```

```
    name: "{{ item }}"
    state: restarted
  with_items: "{{ debian_smb_services }}"
  when: ansible_os_family == 'Debian'

- name: Restart Samba
  service:
    name: "{{ item }}"
    state: restarted
  with_items: "{{ redhat_smb_services }}"
  when: ansible_os_family == 'RedHat'
```

Using Ansible roles

For this section, we are going to use the test folder to test the new role. First, we need to set up the inventory to match our test environment:

```
tests/inventory:
[linuxserver]
node0
node1
node2
```

Then, we edit the test.yml file for the test:

```
tests/test,yml:
- hosts: linuxserver
  remote_user: setup
  become: yes
 roles:
    - samba.lab.edu
```

When executing the test.yml playbook, we need to add to the ansible-playbook command line the -i option and specify the tests/inventory inventory file we filled earlier. The command line should look like the following:

```
ansible-playbook tests/test.yml -i tests/inventory
```

The README.md file can contain some information about the variable of the role to help its users personalize it to their own setup.

 When building mass roles, the best way to test them is to use containers with different base systems.

Summary

In this chapter, we have listed several handy techniques to optimize configuration management coding when using Ansible and other automation tools. We have introduced Ansible roles, including how to make them and how to use them. In Chapter 7, *Ansible Galaxy and Community Roles*, we are going to explore community roles on Ansible Galaxy. We will download and use the highest-rated ones and show how we can add a role on Ansible Galaxy ourselves.

References

Ansible documentation: https://docs.ansible.com/ansible/latest

Ansible Galaxy and Community Roles

7

In the previous chapter, we showed you how to create your own roles, guided by Ansible norms and best practices. There's no need to reinvent the wheel; instead, we can look for what already has been created and use it or alter it to accommodate our needs. This chapter will provide a brief introduction to Ansible Galaxy, both the command and the repository. We will learn how to upload a role that we created to the repository, search for popular community roles to download, set up, and use, and troubleshoot them as well.

This chapter covers the following topics:

- Introduction to Ansible Galaxy
- Uploading a role to Ansible Galaxy
- The best practices of searching for community roles
- Setting up and using a community role
- Troubleshooting a role

Ansible Galaxy

Ansible Galaxy is the platform created by Ansible for its community. It allows its members to make and submit their own roles for other members to use, alter, upgrade, enhance, and optimize.

Ansible Galaxy is built to allow easier role submission by developers and role importation by users. When installing Ansible on the controller host, add in the `ansible-galaxy` command line. This command allows a Terminal interaction with the Ansible Galaxy repository.

Ansible Galaxy has given Ansible a huge advantage and allowed it to grow faster than any other automation tool. The existence of a supply of code written by experienced users is invaluable for less experienced users to easily access and learn from. This supply is composed of well-written Ansible-based projects and workflows.

The Ansible Galaxy hub

The Ansible Galaxy hub is a web portal that hosts an enormous number of community roles. It is categorized into several groups to make searching for a role easier and offers a variety of roles that are developed and maintained by Ansible users. Some roles are better coded and maintained than others. The Ansible Galaxy hub also offers useful information about how to import and use each role, most of which is filled in by its author. Each role should also contain a link to its GitHub project for the source code. As well as this, the information should include the number of downloads, stars, watchers, and forks for each role. The interface also offers a list of all the authors who are signed up to the hub.

Its web interface looks as follows:

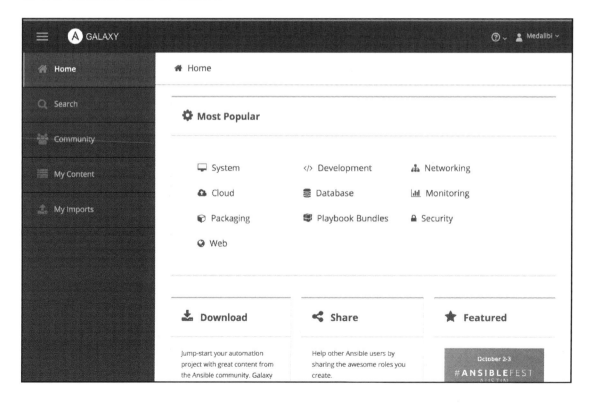

Ansible Galaxy uses GitHub to access an API that requires you to log in to its author or contributor services. By logging in, the interface changes to add a few extra option contributions. The login interface is as follows:

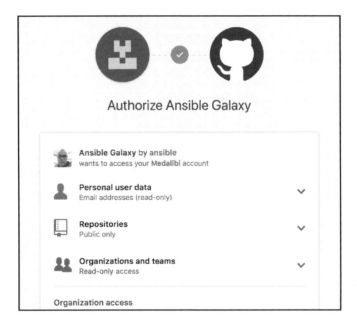

 Ansible does not require authentication to access its roles and use them. The login is only for authors and contributors to be able to submit their code as a contribution to the community.

The Ansible Galaxy repository is organized by tags that indicate the category and service of each role. The tags are not limited to those that are present on the home page. They can be personalized according to the role. However, including one of the home screen tags on your role gives it a much better chance of being found easily.

The Ansible Galaxy command line

The Ansible Galaxy command line `ansible-galaxy` is the tool to be used locally to work on initializing a role.

In the previous chapter, we initiated a role using the option `init`, as shown here:

```
ansible-galaxy init lab-edu.samba
```

This command will create a folder with the name of the role, containing the basic folder and files necessary. These then need to be edited and filled with the appropriate code and files to make the role function.

The Ansible Galaxy command line manages all roles within an Ansible control host. It also allows you to browse roles within the hub. Some of the most frequently used options of this command line are as follows.

The Ansible Galaxy command line allows the removal of one or more roles that are no longer needed from the local Ansible installation using the following command:

```
ansible-galaxy remove lab-edu.ntp
```

It also allows you to search for roles by keywords or tags and see useful information about them, either to double-check their ratings or to learn more about it without using the web interface. This can be done using the following command:

```
ansible-galaxy search geerlingguy.ntp
ansible-galaxy search --galaxy-tags system
ansible-galaxy info geerlingguy.ntp
```

The following screenshot shows a sample output for role information:

```
alibi@alibi-ml ~/vagrant-ansible-lab> ansible-galaxy info geerlingguy.ntp

Role: geerlingguy.ntp
        description: NTP installation and configuration for Linux.
        active: True
        commit: ff09dda458223e2d82ed5a6bfae30dace8b19b3b
        commit_message: PR #46 follow-up: Bump minimum Ansible requirement to 2.4. [ci skip]
        commit_url: https://api.github.com/repos/geerlingguy/ansible-role-ntp/git/commits/ff09dda458223e2d82ed5a6bfae30dace8b19b3b
        company: Midwestern Mac, LLC
        created: 2014-03-05T15:50:12.955490Z
        download_count: 106374
        forks_count: 99
        github_branch: master
        github_repo: ansible-role-ntp
        github_user: geerlingguy
        id: 464
        imported: 2018-08-18T08:04:34.188979-04:00
        is_valid: True
        issue_tracker_url: https://github.com/geerlingguy/ansible-role-ntp/issues
        license: license (BSD, MIT)
        min_ansible_version: 2.4
        modified: 2018-08-18T12:04:34.189259Z
        open_issues_count: 15
        path: [u'/Users/alibi/ansible/roles']
        role_type: ANS
        stargazers_count: 109
        travis_status_url: https://travis-ci.org/geerlingguy/ansible-role-ntp.svg?branch=master
```

If a role found is needed, it can be installed using the `install` option. You can always see the list of installed roles by using the `list` option. The following command shows how this can be done:

```
ansible-galaxy install geerlingguy.ntp
ansible-galaxy list
```

The following screenshot shows an example output for the preceding command:

```
alibi@alibi-ml ~/vagrant-ansible-lab> ansible-galaxy install geerlingguy.ntp
- downloading role 'ntp', owned by geerlingguy
- downloading role from https://github.com/geerlingguy/ansible-role-ntp/archive/1.6.0.tar.gz
- extracting geerlingguy.ntp to /Users/alibi/ansible/roles/geerlingguy.ntp
- geerlingguy.ntp (1.6.0) was installed successfully
alibi@alibi-ml ~/vagrant-ansible-lab> ansible-galaxy list
- geerlingguy.ntp, 1.6.0
- samba.lab.edu, (unknown version)
```

We will discuss further functionalities and options of this command in a later section.

To be able to use a locally created role that has not been uploaded to the Galaxy hub within your Ansible installation, you just need to copy its folder to the assigned role folder within the Ansible configuration.

Ansible is currently developing a new command-line tool called `mazer`. It is an open source project made to manage Ansible content. It is currently an experimental tool that should not replace the `ansible-galaxy` command-line tool.

Galaxy contribution – role importation

The Ansible community impact is very visible with regard to the number and quality of roles that are available for free to the public on the Ansible Galaxy hub. Users from all over the world contribute their code for the good of others. This is the spirit of open source, which has helped to build great tools. Following in the steps of those who have come before us, it is important to contribute every little bit of code that we believe is not available and that may help someone to deal with a challenge.

What to do before role submission

To be able to upload and contribute to Ansible Galaxy, you need to have a GitHub account. This is for two reasons: to log in to the Galaxy hub portal and to upload the role's code as a project to be imported into the Galaxy hub.

Upon first logging into the Ansible Galaxy hub, we are presented with various project access permission configurations. This will allow Galaxy to link the project to your organization.

> The access permission configurations can always be altered later from within the GitHub account option interface.

The **My Content** menu will appear in the Galaxy hub home page. This can be used to list roles that have been written from your account. The menu allows you to add, remove, and edit a version, as well as upgrade roles. It also allows you to add contributors if the roles are being maintained by more than one author. The following screenshot shows what the web interface looks like:

On the local machine, it is advisable that you use a form of Git tool, either the fancy graphical interface that is usually available for macOS and Windows OS or the good old `git` command line. We need to have logged in locally to our GitHub repository for an easier upload:

```
git tag 0.1
git push lab-edu.samba
```

You can always create a role from the GitHub web interface. It can be a bit clumsy to use, but it does the job perfectly.

Role repository

After uploading the code to GitHub, we can now import the role to the Ansible Galaxy hub. From the **My Content** page, choose the **Add Content** button. A box containing all the GitHub projects associated with the account will appear. We select the role we want to import and press **OK**. The menu looks as follows:

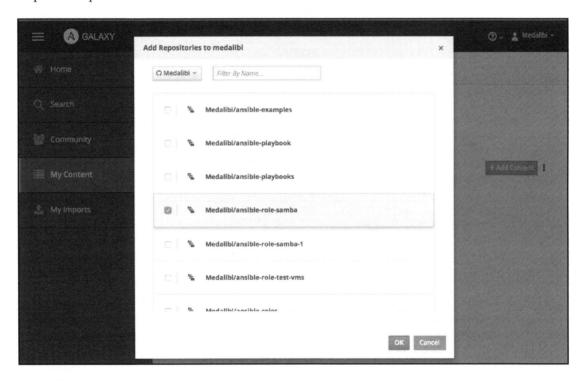

The role then gets added to the list of contents, as shown in the following screenshot:

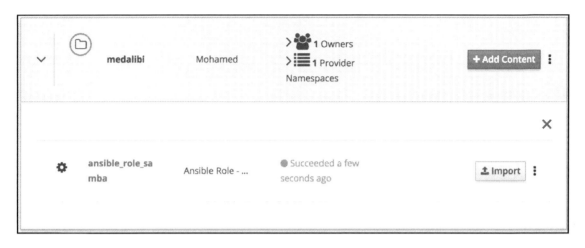

This method allows you to add as many roles as you like to the GitHub account. This step is the actual importation of the role, where the Ansible Galaxy performs some static analysis based on the metadata in the meta folder files.

 After adding a role, we can link organizations that have been imported from our GitHub account. This helps with indicating collaborations and as a search tag.

Each role in a user's account can be managed to add an author and give them certain rights, such as administrator rights. This can be changed in the **Edit property** menu. Any users who are added via this menu have the ability to edit, disable, enable, remove, and update a role and its content.

Finally, the best way to update roles on Galaxy is to set a versioning scheme to their content. This process happens with the help of GitHub tags. Whenever Ansible Galaxy imports a role code from GitHub, it scans the project for tags, looking for a tag that is formatted to hold a versioning syntax.

Ansible Galaxy role management

Let's now discover what the Ansible Galaxy library has to offer. In this section, we are going to explore how to find a role and on what basis we should use it compared to others that have the same function. We will also look at some recommended methods about how to install a role and how to troubleshoot its installation and importation.

Ansible Galaxy role search

In this subsection, we will discuss how to use the Galaxy web portal to find an Ansible role. To do this, we will either use a tag page or the general search page. We recommend using one of the tag pages for a categorized list.

Once we have chosen a category, we can then look at the filters, which are a way of pinpointing specific aspects of a role. The filters that are used by a category can be selected from the drop-down menu. A category can either be a simple keyword, such as **contributor** or **platform**, or it can be a tag. By selecting a category other than a keyword or a tag, we get access to a second drop-down menu that contains all the available options in that category for us to select from.

Filters can be combined, either across category or as multiple entries from the same filter category. This will further narrow down the results that are returned. You can also remove filters that are no longer needed by deleting them from the list of filters underneath the search bar. The filter features can be used on any category page on the portal. It can also be used on the community page where the list of all the authors is held.

Finding a list of roles that match our search does not mean we have finished. We then need to select which role to perform the required task. From the list of roles that match our search, we can use, yet again, the help of other Ansible users. Ansible Galaxy offers a rating system that is composed of different variables. You can tell the quality of a role and how satisfied its users are by looking at how many stars it has. We can also look at how many people are watching the role to follow the changes that are being made, which is a good indication of how well it is being maintained. The number of times a particular role has been downloaded is also useful, but you should compare this with the number of star ratings that have been given because it doesn't show whether a role has been downloaded multiple times by the same user.

Knowing the author of a role is also important. Some Ansible Galaxy authors are known for their high-quality roles and their continuous maintenance.

Ansible Galaxy role installation

We can install Ansible roles in a number of ways. The simplest method is to use the command line with the option `install`, as follows:

```
ansible-galaxy install geerlingguy.ntp
```

Alternatively, we can personalize our installation command by choosing which version we would like from which source. This can be done as follows:

```
ansible-galaxy install geerlingguy.ntp,v1.6.0
ansible-galaxy install
git+https://github.com/geerlingguy/ansible-role-ntp.git
```

We can also install multiple roles at one time using a YAML requirement file. The command line looks as follows:

```
ansible-galaxy install -r requirements.yml
```

The requirements file has a YAML structured file that contains instructions about how to install the different roles required. This is a sample requirements file:

```
# install NTP from Galaxy hub
- src: geerlingguy.ntp

# install Apache from GitHub repo
- src: https://github.com/geerlingguy/ansible-role-apache
  name: apache

# install NFS version 1.2.3 from GitHub
- src: https://github.com/geerlingguy/ansible-role-nfs
  name: nfs4
  version: 1.2.3
```

A requirements file can call other requirements files to install the extra roles that are already stated in the original requirements file. This is shown here:

```
- include: ~/role_req/haproxy_req.yml
```

Another way of installing multiple roles is to rely on the dependency section of the role's `meta` folder. The dependency section follows the same rules as a requirements file when stating the source and version of a certain role.

Ansible Galaxy role troubleshooting

From the user's perspective, setting up roles within the Ansible control machine may cause a few issues that are mainly related either to not having the permissions required to access the role or to the role malfunctioning. The cause of most of those errors is how Ansible is installed. The default Ansible installation puts all its configuration files, inventory, roles, and variables in a root-owned folder (/etc/ansible). Using it as a normal user may, therefore, cause a few issues. This is why we always recommend having a user-personalized Ansible configuration file that points to the folders that the user has access to. Installing a role requires the creation of multiple folders and files; if this is not done in an authorized location, the installation will fail.

We also need to double-check the system requirements of each role. They may need a certain version of Ansible or a certain configuration in a specific file. A role will not work properly if one of their requirements is not properly met.

With regard to importing roles to the Galaxy hub, the main error that users get is failed importation, which usually has something to do with errors in the playbook or in the information about the role that is held in the meta folder. The Galaxy hub gives a detailed log of the error and can even show the exact lines of a specific file where the error has occurred. Once you have fixed the error, you can easily restart the import and continue.

Summary

The Ansible Galaxy hub is a great asset for the accelerated development and success of Ansible. With this resource, most daily tasks have been already converted to organized and resource-optimized roles that are available for public use. In this chapter, we have introduced Ansible Galaxy and covered how to collaborate in the community. We then looked at how to search, install, and troubleshoot roles.

In Chapter 8, *Ansible Advanced Features*, we are going to cover in brief some more advanced features of Ansible that can be handy with regard to security and the needs of more advanced users.

References

Ansible Galaxy documentation: https://galaxy.ansible.com/docs/

Ansible documentation: https://docs.ansible.com/ansible/latest/

8
Ansible Advanced Features

Before finishing this book, we wanted to take a brief look at some of the more interesting and advanced functionalities of Ansible. These can be handy to further enhance your automation. In this chapter, we are going to cover three features: Ansible Vault, and its capacity to increase the security of playbooks and roles; Ansible Container, to enable full container automation with Ansible; and Ansible plugins, with their rich and flexible set of features.

This chapter covers the following topics:

- Overview of Ansible Vault
- How to configure and use Ansible Vault
- Benefits of Ansible Container
- Using Ansible Container
- Overview of Ansible plugins and their features

Ansible Vault

In this section, we are going to introduce the features, use cases, and best practices that are associated with Ansible Vault.

What is Ansible Vault?

Ansible Vault is a tool provided by Ansible that allows its users to encrypt secret variables, which can vary from authentication credentials and keys to sensitive and personal user information. Ansible Vault creates encrypted files to store variables, which can be moved to a secure location if necessary.

Ansible Vault is integrated transparently into the scripts of Ansible roles and playbooks. This means that Vault can encrypt any data structures that are located within those scripts. This includes host and group variables, either stored in the script or from another location imported using the `include_vars` option. They could also be located in the `defaults` or `vars` folder when dealing with an Ansible role. Vault can also encrypt task files when there is a need to hide the name of a particular variable.

Ansible Vault can also be extended to encrypt regular files that are binaries, archives, or text files. This feature is used with file management modules such as `copy`, `unarchive`, and `script`.

Using Ansible Vault

To be able to explore the features of Ansible Vault, we need to make sure we have created at least one encrypted file to store our variables in. For this, we need to use the `ansible-vault` tool as follows:

```
ansible-vault create /home/admin/Vault/vault.yml
```

A password entry prompt will appear, to ask for the password for the newly created Vault file. After typing in the password and confirming it, a new Vault file will be created in the specified location. A default text editor will open for us so that we can fill in the vault file.

Ansible Vault will look for the `EDITOR` environment variable to check which system default text editor is to be used when opening vault files. To use a specific text editor, we need to change the variable on the fly as follows: `export EDITOR=nano; ansible-vault create /home/admin/Vault/vault.yml`.

Any data that is written in the vault file will be encrypted the moment the file gets closed. We can try plotting the content of the text file using the `cat` command–line tool as follows:

```
cat /home/admin/Vault/vault.yml
```

The output of the tool will look as follows:

```
alibi@alibi-ml ~/vagrant-ansible-lab> cat vault.yml
$ANSIBLE_VAULT;1.1;AES256
6165663466333932303535646466303163339303261643562373464656462303836316231653932
30
653834643738663130356234613036653966633313733376303a356132346238393539613631323
065
336563323339353333731356630656636646232633933353386464656131313961393139333366393
5
3866386364316337630a35336235313235386466356233346238336264363339326262333532623
6
6434303535303534306162343037303661666631303964616336623263334636235306431663866
38
62643964373730346566343333335616533316266376531666361
```

The Vault files can only be modified properly using the `ansible-vault` command–line tool. To do this, we need to use the `edit` option, as follows:

> **ansible-vault edit /home/admin/Vault/vault.yml**

After entering the Vault file password chosen during file creation, the default text editor should take over to open the file and show its content in clear text to allow for easier editing. We can also open the vault file in read-only mode using the `view` option:

> **ansible-vault view /home/admin/Vault/vault.yml**

> Running the `ansible-vault` command–line tool using any option will require you to type in the password of the vault file that the action is going to be performed. The vault file password can be edited using the `rekey` option: `ansible-vault rekey /home/admin/Vault/vault.yml`. We need to type in the original password, then the new password, and confirm it.

As we mentioned earlier, Ansible Vault can encrypt and decrypt files when used with file modules. This feature can be used to encrypt files manually and transform them into vault files. It is always possible to manually decrypt them later when necessary. To perform file encryption, we need to use the `encrypt` option for the `ansible-vault` command–line tool.

> **ansible-vault encrypt /home/admin/variables.yml**

This command line will require a password and its confirmation to encrypt and secure the newly converted vault file. This file can be used directly in any playbook shown in the next subsection.

To convert the vault file to a normal text file, we use the same command–line tool with a different option, `decrypt`:

```
ansible-vault decrypt /home/admin/variables.yml
```

After entering the password of the vault file, we should be able to view and edit the file using any tool.

Best practices when using Ansible Vault

Now that we've learned how to create and encrypt vault files, let's look at how to use them properly with Ansible playbooks and roles. To be able to use encrypted variables, we need to provide Ansible with the password for the Vault file. This can be done simply with an interactive prompt when executing the playbook, as follows:

```
ansible-playbook playbook.yml --ask-vault-pass
```

Alternatively, for a more automated method, you could point to the file where the vault password will be stored. This is done as follows:

```
ansible-playbook playbook.yml --vault-password-file
/home/admin/.secrets/vault_pass.txt
```

The file should be a one-line file containing the password as a string. If there is a site vault password, we can always set up a persistent vault password file within the Ansible global configuration file by adding the following line to the `[defaults]` section:

```
vault_password_file = /home/admin/.secrets/vault_pass.txt
```

 From version 2.3, Ansible has introduced a way to encrypt single vault variables. It requires you to use the `encrypt_string` option with the `ansible-vault` command–line tool.

As an example, we are going to use a vault file with a sensitive variable that will get called in a playbook. First, we need to make sure the vault file has the variable properly defined:

```
ansible-vault edit /home/admin/vault.yml
```

We can verify the content of the vault file using the `view` option, as shown in the following screenshot:

```
alibi@alibi-ml ~/vagrant-ansible-lab> ansible-vault view vault.yml
Vault password:
vault_user_pass: P@55w0rd
```

Then, we need to verify that the vault file is included in the playbook and the variable is called:

```
...
   include_vars: /home/admin/vault.yml
   tasks:
     name: connect to a web service
     shell: service-x -user user1 -password "{{ vault_user_pass }}"
...
```

Finally, we execute the playbook while pointing to the location of the vault password file:

```
ansible-playbook service_connect.yml --vault-password-file
/home/admin/.vault
```

It is a good practice to have a set of two variable files located in the usual hosts or group variables folder. You should fill the first file with all the necessary variables, and fill the second one only with the variables that are to be encrypted, by adding a special prefix to their names. Then, adjust the variables in the first file so that they point to the matching prefixed variables in the second file, using Jinja2 syntax. Make sure your second file is encrypted using Ansible Vault. This method causes less hassle when managing many variables that need to be encrypted.

 To enhance the encryption and decryption speed when using Ansible Vault, it is recommended that you have the Python `cryptography` package installed on the system. This can be installed easily using Python PyPI: `pip install cryptography`.

Ansible Container

In this section, we are going to talk about this very handy feature, which is offered by Ansible for its container-focused users.

What is Ansible Container?

Ansible Container is an open source project that helps Ansible users automate the building, deployment, and management of their containers. This feature allows for better container code management when building compose files and allows you to deploy containers on any public or private cloud registries.

With Ansible Container, we can use Ansible features with containers the same way as we can with virtual machines and bare-metal hosts.

Using Ansible Container

Ansible Container is not, by default, installed as part of the Ansible original installation. We need to install it separately on the container host. To simplify the installation, we are going to rely on Python PyPI to install the necessary packages. Ansible Container needs a container engine to work, so we need to specify one during the install process. The following command line shows how we can install Ansible Container with two engines, Docker and Kubernetes:

```
pip install ansible-container[docker,k8s]
```

Ansible Container has a special heavy-lifting container, called the Conductor, which is generated during the build process. The Conductor contains all the necessary dependencies to build a target container image.

The Ansible command line for managing containers, `ansible-container`, offers several functionalities, from development level to testing and production. We use the `init` option to create the container folder and initial configuration files:

```
ansible-container init
```

The following list of files should be present in the directory in which the command line was executed:

```
ansible.cfg
ansible-requirements.txt
container.yml
meta.yml
requirements.yml
.dockerignore
```

The `ansible-container` command line also initiates the container building process by launching the Conductor container to run the instances and base container images that are specified in the `container.yml` file. Then, the Ansible roles that are specified in the file are installed in multiple layers of the container. All of this is done via the container engine. The full command line should look as follows:

`ansible-container build`

We can also orchestrate a container modification that only updates the container image that is affected by the change, without rebuilding all the images, for faster development. Before running the following command, we need to make sure that the change has been made and saved in the `container.yml` file:

`ansible-container run`

Then, to upload and build the container images in a cloud registry, we need to use the `deploy` option. This option also allows you to generate the Ansible code to orchestrate the building of the container images and a production container platform when using Kubernetes or Red Hat OpenShift. The full command line should look as follows:

`ansible-container deploy`

As for the files generated by the `init` option, we can identify the following:

- `container.yml`: This is a YAML file that describes the services of the container, how to build and run the container, and which repositories to push it to.
- `meta.yml`: This contains the necessary information to enable the container project to be shared on Ansible Galaxy.
- `ansible-requirements.yml`: This stores the Python dependencies that are used by the Conductor container when it is built.
- `requirements.yml`: This lists the roles to be used within the container.
- `ansible.cfg`: This contains the Ansible configuration to be followed in the Conductor container.
- `.dockerignore`: This contains the list of files that are irrelevant to the container project. These should be ignored when building and uploading the container project.

Example Ansible container

As an example, we are going to create a simple web server. First, we need to create our Ansible Container folder and the initial configuration files:

```
mkdir /home/admin/Containers/webserver
cd /home/admin/Containers/webserver
ansible-container init
```

Then, we start editing the files that we have created. We start with the container.yml file and fill it with the following code:

```
version: '2'
settings:
  conductor:
    base: 'ubuntu:xenial'
  project_name: webserver

services:
  web:
    from: centos:7
    command: [nginx]
    entrypoint: [/usr/bin/entrypoint.sh]
    ports:
      - 80:80
    roles:
      - nginx-server
```

Then, we fill in the meta.yml file in case we need to upload our container project to Ansible Galaxy. We need to add the following code to it:

```
galaxy_info:
    author: alibi
    description: A generic webserver
    licence: GPL3

    galaxy_tags:
        - container
        - webserver
        - nginx
```

Then, we edit the requirements.txt file and add in the following requirements:

```
nginx-server
```

We will leave the `ansible.cfg`, `.dockerignore`, and `ansible-requirements.yml` files as they are. We do not have anything to change in these files for this container project.

We can now build our container:

```
ansible-container build
```

Ansible plugins

In this section, we are going to briefly introduce Ansible plugins and talk about how we can develop our own.

What are Ansible plugins?

Ansible plugins are pieces of code and functions that add to Ansible's original core functionalities. These plugins enable Ansible to control several APIs and tools that enable the correct functioning of several modules.

The default installation of Ansible includes several essential plugins, which are shown in the following list:

- **Action plugins:** These are frontend plugins for the modules. They can execute actions on the master host before calling the modules themselves.
- **Cache plugins:** These are background plugins that are used to cache host facts. This can help with optimizing fact gathering.
- **Callback plugins:** These help the monitoring and log collection tools to work with Ansible for optimized monitoring.
- **Connection plugins:** These are responsible for communication with remote hosts that support different types of connections.
- **Inventory plugins:** These plugins help generate an inventory from specified hosts.
- **Shell plugins:** These are command controllers that are used to check whether commands are properly formatted and conform with the target machines.
- **Strategy plugins:** These control the execution of Ansible plays and the pipelining of tasks and schedules.
- **Vars plugins:** These inject variables that are defined in the inventory or the group or host variables, but are required for the execution of the task.

Developing Ansible plugins

Ansible does come with many plugins included in its package, but it is always possible to develop our own plugins. This will help extend Ansible's features. Ansible does help developers create new plugins by providing base classes that host several pre-written methods and functions which can be used with new plugins to prevent unnecessary coding. Also, when we have finished writing a plugin, we can easily write a simple unit test for it using Ansible's plugin API.

Summary

In this chapter, we have covered a few handy features offered by Ansible for more advanced uses. We first looked at Ansible Vault, which provides enhanced security during infrastructure automation. We then looked at Ansible Container, which covers the new trend of building and managing containers. Finally, we looked at Ansible plugins and how they allow us to personalize our automation.

With this chapter, we finish our *Ansible QuickStart Guide*. This is not, however, the end of the journey; Ansible has a lot more to offer and the best way to truly master it is to carry out as many projects as possible. There will always be other books, web forums, and blogs to help guide you.

References

Here is the Ansible documentation website: `https://docs.ansible.com/ansible/latest`.

Other Books You May Enjoy

If you enjoyed this book, you may be interested in these other books by Packt:

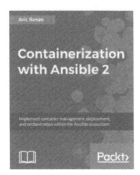

Containerization with Ansible 2

Aric Renzo

ISBN: 978-1-78829-191-0

- Increase your productivity by using Ansible roles to define and build images
- Learn how to work with Ansible Container to manage, test, and deploy your containerized applications.
- Increase the flexibility and portability of your applications by learning to use Ansible
- Discover how you can apply your existing Ansible roles to the image build process
- Get you up and running from building a simple container image to deploying a complex, multi-container app in the cloud.
- Take an indepth look at the architecture of Ansible Container, and learn how to build re-usable container images, reliably and efficiently.

Security Automation with Ansible 2

Madhu Akula, Akash Mahajan

ISBN: 978-1-78839-451-2

- Use Ansible playbooks, roles, modules, and templating to build generic, testable playbooks
- Manage Linux and Windows hosts remotely in a repeatable and predictable manner
- See how to perform security patch management, and security hardening with scheduling and automation
- Set up AWS Lambda for a serverless automated defense
- Run continuous security scans against your hosts and automatically fix and harden the gaps
- Extend Ansible to write your custom modules and use them as part of your already existing security automation programs
- Perform automation security audit checks for applications using Ansible
- Manage secrets in Ansible using Ansible Vault

Leave a review - let other readers know what you think

Please share your thoughts on this book with others by leaving a review on the site that you bought it from. If you purchased the book from Amazon, please leave us an honest review on this book's Amazon page. This is vital so that other potential readers can see and use your unbiased opinion to make purchasing decisions, we can understand what our customers think about our products, and our authors can see your feedback on the title that they have worked with Packt to create. It will only take a few minutes of your time, but is valuable to other potential customers, our authors, and Packt. Thank you!

Index

Y

Made in the USA
San Bernardino, CA
05 December 2018